FROM SLAVERY TO FREEDOM

Our Journey to Freedom and Helping Others
Discover Their Heritage and Identity in Christ

DARYL AND STEPHANIE FITZGERALD

with NEIL T. ANDERSON

FREEDOM IN CHRIST

Published and printed by Freedom In Christ Ministries International 4 Beacontree Plaza, Gillette Way, Reading RG2 0BS, UK. www.freedominchrist.org

First edition 2021

A catalogue record for this book is available from the British Library.

ISBN: 978-1-913082-42-0

Cover Design by Andy Hart.

CONTENTS

QUOTE

God is not interested merely in the freedom of black men, brown men, and yellow men; God is interested in the freedom of the whole human race.[1]

Freedom. True freedom. Everyone longs for it, but most have no idea how to acquire it and live in it. As pastor and Biblical Counselors, Daryl and Stephanie have been on the journey that leads to breaking the internal shackles and laying aside the weights that drag the soul down. Theirs is a message of real hope grounded in the knowledge of Who can set you free and how you can proactively participate with the Holy Spirit and experience the freedom God wants to bring into your life. Stephanie and Daryl unpack with clarity the steps you can take as you travel with Christ on your journey towards true freedom with honesty, transparency, and grace.

—BRUCE FIDLER
Global Manager—Leadership 215; Every Nation Churches & Ministries | www.leadership215.com

One of the best ways to learn is to be SILENT and LISTEN. I've been doing a lot of that lately ... talking less and listening more. In reading this book, you have the opportunity to do the same. In *From Slavery to Freedom*, as coaches, church leaders, and consultants, my friends Daryl and Stephanie Fitzgerald share their stories and their personal journeys to freedom. There is much wisdom to glean from their lives. They have experienced true freedom... the only lasting freedom... freedom in Christ.

As a coach and consultant to pastors and churches, I have the privilege of serving churches all over the nation. Sadly, most churches are full of people who live in bondage, addiction, and all manner of sin. Too few churches emphasize one of the primary ministries of Jesus' life—He died to save us, heal us, and set us free!

1

It's been said that free people free people. Never has that statement been more accurate than with this incredible couple. You will discover that Daryl's and Stephanie's lives are contagious with the message of freedom. If you apply the principles imparted here, you too can be completely free.

—ED FUNDERBURK

Executive Director, Ed Funderburk Ministries | edfunderburk.cc
Former Executive Pastor, Gateway Church-Dallas Fort Worth

"The LORD works righteousness and justice for all the oppressed" (Psalm 103:6).

The unresolved realities of racial injustice, systemic discrimination, and cultural bias are issues that can only be solved by a righteous God who inspires wisdom and action in and through His redeemed people. Daryl and Stephanie Fitzgerald not only know the liberating truth of freedom in Christ but contextualize that message in a way that brings hope to race relations and reconciliation. *From Slavery to Freedom* is healing salve to the soul for people of color who have experienced racial trauma and forms of race-based stress. As a Caucasian follower of Jesus Christ, I personally find this book to be a call to understanding, repentance, and humility for white evangelicals. In Christ, the racial barriers that have separated the family of God for far too long can be demolished with truth and grace—that is the person of Jesus Christ. I consider this a must-read book that elevates the notion of reconciliation far above the societal discord that fills the airwaves.

—CHRIS CAMPBELL

M.A.B.S.; M.A.P.C.; L.P.C.; Founder of Generation Freedom and
President of Resolutions Counseling Inc | www.generationfreedom.org

Knowing Daryl and Stephanie's heart and passion for true freedom in the area of racial tension, I can honestly say this book is "for such a time as this". As you blend the real life stories and experiences with the practical and timeless steps the Bible outlines for freedom, I believe this book will heal many people on all sides. However you have been affected by racism, God has an answer for your questions. I think this book will help many get to the root of the issue and no longer just treat the symptoms. Fitzgeralds' story lines up with their mission...to see all people be brought together in wholeness as sons and daughters of our Father God.

—MARK RAMPULLA
Senior Pastor, Southview Church | southview.cc

Daryl and Stephanie Fitzgerald are the real deal in heart and spirit. They know what fighting for their freedom looks like, and in the pages of their new book with Neil Anderson, *"From Slavery to Freedom,"* they share with vulnerability and wisdom how they found freedom and how your heart can too. Their lives are evidence that, "he whom the Son sets free is free indeed."

—DENISE HILDRETH JONES
President & Founder of Reclaiming Hearts Ministries
www.reclaiminghearts.org

Since the Bible contains all the information we need to be transformed and step into the abundant life, why is it so rare to find a Christian truly walking in freedom? With more access to Bible commentaries, sermons, and Christian books than any generation before us, why are we still chained to our old flesh patterns? I think there is a fundamental gap in the discipleship process experienced by most Christians in the Western world. The discipleship strategies Daryl and Stephanie include in this book address that gap while acknowledging that only true repentance and the power of God are responsible for the transformation. Their approach is challenging but not abrasive; compassionate, but not sentimental. Get a copy for yourself, your pastor, and one to loan out to all the friends you'll tell about this book!

—RAMIRO AND MELISSA CRUZ
Pastors of Mosaico Church | mosaicochurch.com

Daryl and Stephanie are great Biblical counselors and ministers. And *From Slavery to Freedom* is an essential and timely book. I have known this powerful couple for years and have seen the experience, wisdom, and deep compassion they both have for people to experience the life that Jesus paid for all of us to have. They can genuinely help people thrive. And they can equip those of us who seek to help people succeed. I can't wait to apply the deep insights from this terrific book and these terrific ministers into my counseling practice.

—KEITH TOWER
Senior Pastor, HighPoint Church; Clinical Director, HighPoint Counseling; Executive Director, HighPoint Consulting

As a doctor and practitioner, I understand the mental and emotional bondage that anxiety, depression, and fear have on those who desire to find peace and freedom. The physical effects at times can be debilitating. But there is a spiritual side to anxiety, depression, and fear that is often a missing ingredient that can aid in the healing process. Daryl and Stephanie Fitzgerald address and bring a much-needed spiritual perspective that can help resolve the mental and emotional struggles that plague many who deal with mental health. Freedom is possible because Christ offers us freedom through His blood. It's our gracious inheritance.

—DR. ASA T. BRIGGS
DNP – Clinical Assistant Professor, Clemson University

This book is a must-read for anyone who truly wants to "experience" the freedom that comes with understanding "who we are in Christ." Daryl and Stephanie give us great principles from God's Word and their personal experiences on how we can "possess" the freedom that God has for us because of our true identity. The authors encourage us that we can possess what we confess when we move from belief words we agree with to conviction words we live by. Transformation happens when information goes from revelation to application.

—SHERMAN SMITH
NFL Running Backs Coach, Super Bowl Champion Seattle Seahawks

As a professional coach in the NFL, I can only point my players in the right direction. Daryl and Stephanie have pointed us in the right direction in this book. I can identify with the pain from reading their stories. I grew up in a family where life was not easy. Sometimes life can make you feel like you are the only one who grew up in a challenging family environment but reading the stories in their book let me know that I am not alone. The keys to success and freedom in life are realizing and understanding your identity in Christ and knowing God as a loving heavenly Father. In Christ, we have the answers for dealing with the fear and anxiety we all face in this world.

—TIM WALTON
NFL Defensive Backs Coach, Jacksonville Jaguars

From Slavery to Freedom is a book that shows us how to win in this game of life. It addresses many of the issues facing the African-American community. The testimonies and stories from Daryl and Stephanie empower us to break free from the guilt and shame of our past actions and walk in the freedom that Christ purchased for us. As a professional athlete, I've been blessed to learn from some great men/brothers inside the locker room. In addition to those lessons, the lessons and advice my wife and I have learned from Daryl and Stephanie have been invaluable.

—WESLEY WOODYARD
NFL Linebacker, Tennessee Titans

ACKNOWLEDGMENTS

We are grateful for the many people who have encouraged us to write this book, to persevere through the ups and downs of writing, and to finally bring it to life. We would like to thank our parents who did their best to teach us the importance of our faith. We would like to thank our children: Ashley, Shayna, Darius, Alexis, and Alexandria. You guys are our gifts! Thank you for giving us the privilege to love and walk with you as your parents. Thank you for allowing us to counsel you and teach you the principles of who you are in Christ. We pray and encourage you to go out and change the world for the Kingdom of God! Thank you to all of our supporters and partners who have believed in us. You have given of your time and treasure so that we are able to help bring hope and healing to hurting humanity.

We want to thank Dr. Neil T. Anderson for discipling, mentoring, and inviting us to come on staff with Freedom in Christ Ministries. Our pursuit to live a life of freedom was born many years ago at one of Dr. Anderson's first conferences in Nashville, Tennessee. When Stephanie and I heard the message of Freedom in Christ, it changed the trajectory of our marriage and family. However, we had no idea that it would lead to our meeting Dr. Anderson and building a relationship and friendship that would lead us to publish our first book with him. He not only permitted us to adapt material from his many books, but he also assisted us in writing our story. Neil, as he prefers to be called, wants all the staff of Freedom in Christ Ministries to have ownership of the message. It is our message, and we want the whole body of Christ to embrace the truth that believers are children of God and that it was for freedom that Christ set them free. We would like to thank the U.S. staff of Freedom in Christ Ministries and the staff of Freedom In Christ Ministries International who published and believe in this project.

> **"** WHEN IT COMES TO RACISM, AS A CITIZEN OF THE KINGDOM OF HEAVEN, MY PHYSICAL HERITAGE AS AN AFRICAN AMERICAN SHOULD NOT GUIDE MY DECISIONS AS A BELIEVER; MY SPIRITUAL HERITAGE AS A BELIEVER SHOULD GUIDE MY DECISIONS AS AN AFRICAN AMERICAN. **"**

Dr. Martin Luther King is quoted saying, "God is not interested merely in the freedom of black men and brown men, and yellow men; God is interested in the freedom of the whole human race." With all of the racial tension surrounding our country, we understand how crucially important it is that people know that the answer to racism is the good news of the Gospel of Jesus Christ. As an African American living in the United States of America, I understand what it feels like to experience the sting of racism. However, when it comes to racism, as a citizen of the Kingdom of Heaven, my physical heritage as an African American should not guide my decisions as a believer; my spiritual heritage as a believer should guide my decisions as an African American. Therefore, as a child of God, my voice must echo the voice of my heavenly Father. We are all equally created in the image of God, and the death, burial, resurrection, and ascension of Jesus Christ makes it possible for us to be reconciled to one another. God's answer to any form of prejudice or racism starts with forgiving each other, just as in Christ God forgave us (see Ephesians 4:32).

A well-known American abolitionist and political activist, Harriet Tubman, was born into slavery. However, she did not allow the culture in which she lived or the society in which she was raised to stop her from pursuing freedom for herself, her family, and over 300 other African Americans. She went on nineteen journeys to rescue these men and women of African descent from the bondage of physical slavery. She was given the nickname Moses because she led her family and friends from slavery to freedom. Stephanie and I want to do our part to lead as many men and women as possible from the chains of spiritual slavery to spiritual freedom, which is only found in Christ. We can walk freely from the sin of racism and any other sins because we have put on the new self who is being renewed to a true knowledge according to the image of the One who created us (Colossians 3:10). We understand that these issues can only be resolved in Christ. As people read our story and the story of others whom we have helped, we hope that it might play a small part in helping you overcome the challenges of racism, depression, sexual addiction, marital conflict, and other issues of the heart. We pray that you find the hope of Christ as you read our journey from slavery to freedom.

—Daryl & Stephanie

Overcoming Religion and Racism

DARYL'S STORY

Slaves first set foot in Virginia in the year 1619, two hundred miles from where I was raised. My great-great-grandmother Pattie Wimbush Fitzgerald's father was between the ages of nine and twelve years old when he was sold into slavery. He was purchased for $300.00. My great-great-grandfather, Bose Fitzgerald, was born April 6th, 1876, a few short years after Abraham Lincoln issued the Emancipation Proclamation declaring that all slaves of African descent were free. I was born more than a century after the Emancipation Proclamation was passed into law. However, because of the lingering effects of slavery in the form of discrimination, social injustice, segregation, and Jim Crow laws, many in the African American community went from experiencing physical slavery to mental and emotional slavery. We continued to face the mental and emotional stress of living in a country where most of society devalued our presence.

Railroad tracks, cemeteries, and churches separated black and white communities, and it seemed that I was born on the wrong side of the divide. Schools were integrated, but we all felt safer sitting and playing

Bose Fitzgerald
My Great-Great-Grandfather

Pattie Wimbush Fitzgerald
My Great-Great-Grandmother

with our own people during lunch and recess. Attending church was mandatory for me then since my stepfather was in leadership. He now pastors his own church. We sang a lot of old "Negro spirituals," which seemed depressing to me because I did not understand that they were born out of hardship from slavery with hidden messages of freedom and a longing for heaven, or the "Promised Land."

We weren't rich, but our physical needs were taken care of, and for that I am grateful. I wish I could say that our family was an emotionally close-knit group that demonstrated love and affection, but it was not. My parents loved me as best they knew how and worked hard to provide for my physical needs, but providing healthy emotional support was something of a foreign concept in our home. It seemed like I could never live up to my parents' expectations when at home, playing sports, or attending church. Growing up in a community where discrimination and racism existed was also difficult. As an African American, you knew where you were welcomed in a society filled with prejudice and hate.

EARLY BATTLES OF DISCRIMINATION

I recall an incident in the third grade when I was anxiously waiting for the lunch bell to ring. In anticipation, our teacher walked to the doorway and stood there to make sure we were properly lined up. We sat on the edge of our seats, ready to rush the doorway, hoping to be the first in line. On this particular day, I was the first in line and felt very excited about it. I looked at the teacher seeking her approval, but the look on her face was cold and hard as a stone. She wouldn't even make eye contact with me, leaving me to wonder what I had done wrong. I suddenly felt very uncomfortable being at the front of the line. When everybody was ready, she turned and walked toward the cafeteria. After walking down a flight of stairs, she stopped and kicked me with the back of her heel! I felt totally humiliated. I believed that she was sending the message that I had no business being in the front of the line trying to lead because of the color of my skin. Feeling embarrassed, I told my parents about what happened, and they questioned the school about the incident. Occurrences like this were common growing up as an African American in the United States. I struggled emotionally with feelings of insecurity, insignificance, and acceptance. I had recurring thoughts like, "I'm not good enough," and "being white is better than being black." I developed an inferiority complex and a poor sense of worth.

SPIRITUAL ATTACKS AND THE CHURCH

Growing up as a part of a church community was not without its challenges. When I was in my pre-teen years, a church in our community was promoting a "must-see" movie on the subject of hell. All of my friends were curious about the movie and asked if I was attending. Although I didn't want to go, I reluctantly agreed because I didn't want to give the impression that I was afraid. The movie was filled with scenes describing what would happen to people if they went to hell. I was terrified after seeing how Satan was portrayed in the movie. I developed an unhealthy fear of the devil and demons. I began looking over my shoulder, fearful that Satan was after me, especially at night. I didn't like being home alone because sometimes it felt like something else was in the house with me. Sometimes I dreaded going to bed at night because I was afraid that I might die in my sleep and demons would drag me off to hell.

> **THERE WAS AN INVISIBLE BATTLE GOING ON IN THE SPIRITUAL WORLD FOR MY MIND, AND SATAN WAS USING RACISM AND DISCRIMINATION AS A TOOL TO HAVE ME BELIEVE THAT MY WORTH AND VALUE WAS BASED ON THE COLOR OF MY SKIN.**

To alleviate the fear, I would sleep with the light on at night and turn on the radio to drown out fearful thoughts. I was often abruptly awakened at precisely 3 a.m. with a sense of dread and wondered why it was always 3 a.m. One night I heard an eerie song on the radio and saw the silhouette of a black figure standing in front of my bed. I closed my eyes in fear, hoping that it was just my imagination, but it was still there when I opened my eyes. Not wanting to believe what I was seeing, I closed my eyes again, but I could still see the image in my mind. That is when I panicked! My thoughts began racing, and my heart sank with fear. I knew I was going to be taken to hell by this "thing." I wanted to run out of my room, but I was too afraid to move. That dark figure started walking toward me until it was about a foot away and then just disappeared.

I stayed awake the rest of the night, anxiously waiting to see the light of day. Fear became the primary reason why I attended church, but if I brought up the subject of the devil, demons, or hell, all I ever heard from people in the church was "Don't mess with Satan." I got the impression that he was just as powerful as God and apparently more present in my experience. I realized that people in the church were just as afraid of the devil as I was!

My church experiences and my experiences with racism weighed heavily on me mentally and emotionally. I thought from a very young age, "I'm not going to stay in this small town," but I had no idea how I was going to get out. The one thing I was good at was sports, so I pursued that, hoping it would lead me to a better life.

STEPHANIE'S STORY

I was born in Hickory, North Carolina, but I didn't live there very long. I was three years old when my parents divorced. My mother, three brothers, and I moved to Los Angeles, California in 1968, a pivotal year in the civil rights movement. The Black Panthers had a shootout with police in Oakland, California. Robert F. Kennedy was assassinated in Los Angeles, and Martin Luther King was assassinated in Memphis. The whole country was struggling with racial tensions. I attended a predominantly black elementary school where students came from all walks of life, but most were like me. We lived in single-parent homes with mothers who were doing all they could to provide for their children. Since most of my friends didn't have a father in their home, growing up without a father seemed like the norm, so it was never discussed. My family of five was very close, and we enjoyed doing life together.

My home and the school I attended were located in a part of Los Angeles known for gang violence. Feeling unsafe, I often ran home after school, and I was taught to be alert and pay attention to my surroundings at all times. When I was in elementary school, I didn't think I would live long enough to be an adult. On my way home from school one day, I noticed that the front door of a building was open, and, for some unknown reason, I ventured in. I said "Hi" to a man on a ladder who said "Hi" back, and I asked, "What are you doing?" He said, "I'm doing some repairs. This is a church. Do you go to church?" I said, "No." He said, "Well go home and tell your mom and dad to bring you to church this Sunday at 10 a.m." I said, "My daddy doesn't live with us." He responded, "Well, tell your mother to bring you to church." I said, "Okay!" Church? What was the church? I had no clue, but there was something about that man on the ladder that made me want to go.

I told my mother what the man on the ladder said. Mom didn't take us, but the following Sunday she gave my three brothers and me some money for an offering and sent us to church, where I discovered that the man on the ladder was the pastor. We enjoyed going to church. We met new friends who became like family. We were active in the church, sang in the choir, participated in plays, and enjoyed Vacation Bible School. One Sunday, the pastor said, "You kids can't come back unless you bring your mother." I was devastated because I liked going to church. As soon as we got home, I said, "Mom, you have to go to church with us," and my brothers chimed in with agreement. To my surprise, my mother said, "Yes." It was the first time my mother attended the church, but our family joined New Pleasant Hill Missionary Baptist Church that Sunday.

I was bused to Mulholland Jr. High School in middle school and experienced a very different culture. Most of the students didn't look or talk like me and didn't have the same family structure. As I rode the school

> **GROWING UP IN THE AFRICAN AMERICAN COMMUNITY, WE UNDERSTOOD THE SIGNIFICANCE OF BEING "IN CHURCH," BUT WE DID NOT UNDERSTAND THE SIGNIFICANCE OF BEING "IN CHRIST."**

bus, I stared at the beautiful homes in that part of town. I dreamt about living in one of those houses in an area that appeared to be fun, friendly, and, most importantly, free of gang violence.

The effort to force integration by busing black students to predominantly white schools may have been well-intentioned, but not all resident teachers and students were receptive. I was eleven years old and wasn't mature enough to process the racial attitudes we faced. Initially, my friends who were bused with me banded together, and we refused to be intimidated by our new surroundings. Fortunately, I got involved in extracurricular activities where racial diversity was tolerated. I slowly began to make friends with white students. Some even invited me to their homes.

IN CHURCH BUT NOT IN CHRIST

Daryl and I were "in church," but we weren't "in Christ." Growing up in the African American community, we understood the significance of being "in church," but we did not understand the significance of being "in Christ." Attending church is a great practice, but walking into a church building does not mean that you get to go to heaven and that you are not a slave to sin or Satan. We have never actually been slaves like our ancestors in the conventional sense of the word, but we were slaves to sin like all people who are born dead in their trespasses and sins (see Ephesians 2:1). It doesn't make any difference on which side of the tracks one is born. "All of us also lived among them at one time, gratifying the cravings of our flesh and following its desires and thoughts. Like the rest, we were by nature deserving of wrath" (Ephesians 2:3). As believers, we have spiritually, mentally, and emotionally been set free, and we no longer think, feel, or live like slaves.

> **WE HAVE NEVER ACTUALLY BEEN PHYSICAL SLAVES LIKE OUR ANCESTORS IN THE CONVENTIONAL SENSE OF THE WORD, BUT WE WERE SPIRITUAL SLAVES TO SIN LIKE ALL PEOPLE WHO ARE BORN DEAD IN THEIR TRESPASSES AND SINS (SEE EPHESIANS 2:1). IT DOESN'T MAKE ANY DIFFERENCE ON WHICH SIDE OF THE TRACKS ONE IS BORN.**

The apostle Paul wrote, "It was for freedom that Christ set us free" (Galatians 5:1). "But now that you have been set free from sin and have become slaves of God, the benefit you reap leads to holiness, and the result is eternal life. For the wages of sin is death, but the gift of God is eternal life in Christ Jesus our Lord" (Romans 6:22, 23). You might be thinking, "I want to know more about this freedom because I don't feel very free." Perhaps a story of freedom will help, one that our ancestors certainly struggled with.

Slavery in the United States was abolished by the Thirteenth Amendment on December 18th, 1865. How many slaves were there on December 19th? In reality, there were none, but many still lived like slaves because the truth was hidden from them.

Suppose several plantation owners were devastated by the Emancipation Proclamation: "We're ruined! Slavery has been abolished. We've lost the battle to keep our slaves." Their chief spokesman slyly responded, "Not necessarily. As long as these people think they are still slaves, the Emancipation Proclamation will have no practical effect. We don't have a legal right over them anymore, but many of them don't know it. Keep your slaves from learning the truth, and your control over them will not even be challenged."

One cotton farmer asked, "But what if the news spreads?"

"Don't panic. We have another barrel on our gun. We may not be able to keep them from hearing the news, but we can still keep them from understanding it. They don't call me the father of lies for nothing (see John 8:44). We still have the potential to deceive the whole world (see Revelation 12:9). Just tell them they misunderstood the Thirteenth Amendment. Tell them that they are going to be free not that they are free already. The truth they heard is just 'positional' truth, not the actual truth. Someday they may receive the benefits, but not now."

"But they will expect me to say that. They won't believe me."

"Then pick a few persuasive ones who are convinced that they're still slaves and let them do the talking for you. Remember, most of these newly freed people were born slaves and have lived like slaves their whole lives. All we have to do is deceive them so that they still think like slaves. As long as they continue to do what slaves do, it will not be hard to convince them that they must still be slaves. They will maintain their slave identity because of the things they do. The moment they try to profess that they are no longer slaves, just whisper in their ear, 'How can you even think you are no longer a slave when you are still doing things that slaves do?' After all, we have the capacity to accuse the brethren day and night."

Years later, many African descendants had still not heard the wonderful news that they had been freed. Naturally, they continued to live the way they had always lived. Some heard the good news, but they told themselves, "I'm still living like a slave, doing the same things I have always done. My experience tells me that I must not be free. Everything is the same as before the Proclamation, so it must not be true. I must still be a slave." So, they continued as if they had not received freedom!

Then one day, a former slave heard the good news and received it with great joy. He checked out the validity of the Proclamation and discovered that the highest of all authorities originated the decree. Not only that, but it personally cost that authority a tremendous price so that slaves could be free. The slave's life was transformed. He reasoned that it would be hypocritical to continue living as a slave, even though his feelings told him he still was. Determined to live by what he knew to be true, his experiences began to change dramatically. He realized that his old master had no authority over him and did not need to be obeyed. He gladly serves the one who set him free.[1]

As you read that story, what stood out? Did you see how easily deception can keep you in bondage to a life of a slavery even though you are free? Do you see yourself acting like a slave even though you have been made free? Do you see that the battle of racism, slavery, and prejudice is a spiritual battle? In order to win this battle, you must know the truth. Our fight is not against flesh and blood, church, religion, racism, or any other "-isms," but against Satan (see Ephesians 6:12). When Adam chose to sin against the command of God in the Garden of Eden, all of humanity became slaves to Satan, sin, and death. God never wanted people to be enslaved. However, spiritual and physical slavery results from disobedience to God.

When Adam and Eve sinned, they died spiritually; they were separated from God, and the entire human race would suffer. There were no laws to govern man's behavior because when Adam and Eve chose to rebel against God's command, they decided to live their lives independent of God. "Then the Lord saw that the wickedness of man was great on the earth and that every intent of the thoughts of his heart was only evil continually" (Genesis 6:5 NASB). To help correct that, God graciously established the Old Testament Covenant of Law. However, nobody could live up to it because the Law could not impart life (Galatians 3:21), and that is what Adam and Eve lost in the Garden of Eden. The Pharisees added to the Law many restrictions (dos and don'ts) in an attempt to keep people from breaking the Law. However, those restrictions only led to legalism, a burden that people could not live up to. Introducing the Law in the Old Testament did lead to a more civilized culture, but it didn't change the nature of humanity.

In a similar fashion, when there were no laws in opposition to slavery against African Americans, evil people took advantage of defenseless men and women for selfish gain. Thankfully the Thirteenth Amendment and Civil Rights Laws were enacted to put a legal end to slavery and Jim Crow laws. The Civil Rights movement of the 1960s did improve social justice, but it didn't improve the condition of human hearts. Since racism and legalism still persist in church and society, should we take a Pharisaical position of enacting more laws believing that conditions will improve through social action and political maneuvering? In reality, a legalistic-driven church can cause more harm than good because it tends to be judgmental. Affirmative action was enacted as law to ensure that qualified African American applicants were given the same equal opportunities for employment as everyone else. Still, it has become divisive because it appears to favor one group of people over the other. Is that really the answer to the problem?

Those laws (and any laws) are powerless to change human hearts or give us eternal life. Changing the law may superficially alter behavior, but it will not do away with the problem of sin or change the human heart's natural condition. That will only happen when people genuinely repent by putting their hope and faith in God and have a clear understanding of who they are in Christ. As believers, "Do we not all have one Father? Did not one God create us? Why do we profane the covenant of our ancestors by being unfaithful to one another?" (Malachi 2:10)

In the next chapter, we will share our journey from slavery to freedom in Christ. My heritage and identity go much deeper than my skin tone and my historical roots as an African American. I don't deny my heritage as an African American, but my physical heritage as an African American does not define who I am. Instead, my spiritual heritage as a child of God defines who I am, gives me purpose, and shapes my identity. We "have put on the new self who is being renewed to a true knowledge according to the image of the One who created him—a renewal in which there is no distinction between Greek and Jew, circumcised and uncircumcised, Barbarian, Scythian, slave, and freeman, but Christ is all and in all" (Colossians 3:10, 11 NASB). We are children of God, and so is every born-again believer. That is the only means by which we can overcome racism, sexism, and elitism.

> **MY HERITAGE AND IDENTITY GO MUCH DEEPER THAN MY SKIN TONE AND MY HISTORICAL ROOTS AS AN AFRICAN AMERICAN. I DON'T DENY MY HERITAGE AS AN AFRICAN AMERICAN, BUT MY PHYSICAL HERITAGE AS AN AFRICAN AMERICAN DOES NOT DEFINE WHO I AM. INSTEAD, MY SPIRITUAL HERITAGE AS A CHILD OF GOD DEFINES WHO I AM, GIVES ME PURPOSE, AND SHAPES MY IDENTITY.**

Chapters Two through Four will share the core message of Freedom in Christ Ministries. We believe that every church can be equipped to set its people free and heal the wounds of the broken-hearted.

After discipling hundreds of people, we have found one common denominator for all those who struggle in their faith: none of them knew who they were in Christ, nor did they understand what it meant to be a child of God. Since the Holy Spirit is bearing witness with our spirits that we are children of God (see Romans 8:16), why didn't they sense that, "Yet to all who did receive him, to those who believed in his name, he gave the right to become children of God" (John 1:12)? Why didn't they know that?

Chapter Five shares a strategy for setting your people free. We are not offering a new counseling technique or to be church consultants. Freedom comes through genuine repentance and faith in God. He is the Wonderful Counselor and the only One who can set people free and bring lasting healing to mental, emotional, and spiritual wounds.

The remaining chapters describe how the message of freedom can overcome anger, anxiety, depression, sexual addiction, chemical addiction, dysfunctional relationships, and more. Today people inside and outside of the church are plagued with unresolved spiritual and emotional conflicts. These conflicts can play a part in how mentally and emotionally unstable they are as individuals. We believe Christ really is the answer, and these issues can be resolved through genuine repentance and faith in God. God has worked wonders in our lives, and we have seen Him do the same in the people we minister to when they choose to walk by faith and believe the truth of God's Word.

CHAPTER 1

Overcomers: Our Journey to Freedom

DARYL'S STORY

I am thankful that I grew up in church, but going to church was challenging. My church experience was more of a religious performance than a spiritual encounter with the living God. My motivation for attending church was based on tradition, religious duties, performance, fear, and avoiding punishment, not on knowing Jesus. I heard many dos and don'ts on what to do to please God. This led me to believe that in order to be loved by God, I had to do the right thing. I felt like everything in my life had to be all together in order to be accepted by God. As a result, I began to drift away mentally and emotionally from home and church because it seemed like I could never live up to the expectations of being holy.

I always loved sports, and my stepfather refereed sports games in our community. Since he was connected to the local schools, he knew the basketball coach at a private school. He saw an opportunity for me to play basketball and obtain a better education, and he asked me if I would like to attend. It was a turning point in my life. It exposed me to a different culture. I started on the varsity basketball team for three years and began to develop relationships with those who lived on the other side of the tracks. I recognized that not all white people were racist.

There is a common phrase in the African American culture that says, "What goes on in the house stays in the house." When I was young, I was sexually molested. I remember being threatened not to say anything. As a seven year old child, I was afraid. I didn't know what to do, so I never told anyone. I felt a tremendous amount of guilt and shame because of what happened. I thought, "What was wrong with me? Why would this happen to me?" In my pre-teen years, I began to be sexually active to try to prove my masculinity and self-worth. My unhealthy sexual appetite grew and lasted throughout my high school years.

> **" I HEARD MANY DOS AND DON'TS ON WHAT TO DO TO PLEASE GOD. THIS LED ME TO BELIEVE THAT IN ORDER TO BE LOVED BY GOD, I HAD TO DO THE RIGHT THING. "**

My basketball skills led to a scholarship to Liberty University. I thought I was on my way out of my old life, but my old life caught up with me. My sexual behavior continued halfway through my freshman year at LU until I was found out. To my shock, I was called into the Dean's office and told that I was being dismissed from the school and cut from the basketball team. They had me call my parents, inform them of what I had done and what the consequences were. I had no desire to go home, but I had no other choice. I thought my life was over! Since I was out of school, I resolved that I would get a job working in the local factory and do drugs like others in my community. Then a miracle happened! In early December I received a call from Liberty University that I was reinstated with my scholarship to play basketball. I still don't know what prompted that, but I was grateful for the second chance. Near the beginning of the spring semester, an evangelist named Bailey Smith spoke to the student body on the college campus. It was like I heard a clear presentation of who Jesus was for the first time. The idea that God loved me, accepted me, and gave his life for me was different from how I viewed God. I believed that if I sinned God was angry and disappointed with me and was waiting to punish me for sinning. Somehow I missed the story of the Gospel that Jesus came to die for my sin. I finally understood I was valuable enough to God that He came to take away my sin, not to punish me for sinning. Hearing a clear presentation of the love of God gave me a different perspective of Him and made me feel that my life mattered.

After finishing my first semester, I stayed in Lynchburg, VA. Then I blew out my knee while playing in a basketball pickup game. They put 27 pins in my knee during surgery and started me on rehab, but my zeal for basketball was gone. I didn't want to play anymore. For several weeks I battled whether I should give up my childhood dream. I finally decided to tell the coach that I was done. After making that decision, a huge burden was lifted. I could not believe how much peace I felt after leaving his office. Like a loving father, God started me on a journey to freedom that showed me how much He truly cared for me. I was finally being set free from the bondage of being accepted based on my performance. During that time, I started experiencing God's love and kindness in ways I had never experienced before.

> **" SOMEHOW I MISSED THE STORY OF THE GOSPEL THAT JESUS CAME TO DIE FOR MY SIN. I FINALLY UNDERSTOOD I WAS VALUABLE ENOUGH TO GOD THAT HE CAME TO TAKE AWAY MY SIN, NOT TO PUNISH ME FOR SINNING. "**

When I gave up playing basketball, I no longer had a scholarship. As a result, I was billed $8,400 for the fall semester, which I could not pay, so I sat out and worked. During that time of transition in my life, I met Chris Williamson and Andre Sims, and together we formed a Christian hip hop group and started doing street evangelism in the inner city. People noticed our passion, and that led to invitations from other cities across the country. Word got back to the late Dr. Jerry Falwell, the Chancellor at Liberty University, who called us into his office. He said, "I have done some things in the African American community that I deeply regret. I would like to help you in any way I can." We were stunned when he offered us a full scholarship through a master's degree, which we gladly accepted.

STEPHANIE'S STORY

The pastor and his wife in California became second parents to my siblings and me. If my mom needed help, they were always there. I remember memorizing the books of the Bible and feeling very accomplished for reciting all sixty-six books in order, but I could not have told anyone the content of those books. At the time, I couldn't have shared a clear presentation of the Gospel, and I knew nothing of God's unconditional love. What I did understand was the basic dos and don'ts of church life. For example, you don't have sex, don't drink, and don't curse or use foul language, and you do attend church regularly, go to Sunday School, participate in activities of the church, and bring money to give your offering.

After living in Los Angeles for almost 16 years, we moved back to North Carolina, and I was heartbroken. I remember riding to the airport with several cars trailing us filled with friends who came to say goodbye. We all stood in disbelief and cried and hugged over and over again until we had no choice but to board the plane. I wondered if I would ever see them again. Moving back to North Carolina meant a new beginning that I was not excited about, but not having to deal with gang violence brought some consolation to my dreadful situation.

Being the new kid on campus in the South was a culture shock at first. I found myself feeling the sting of racism like when I was in middle school. It was clear that some students and teachers felt that white people should stay with white people and black people need to stay with black people.

My great-grandmother attended a Presbyterian church, and I occasionally went with her, but the church wasn't an integral part of our family experience like it was in California. Being an honor student, a pageant queen, and an athlete opened up opportunities for meeting new people. That's how I met my boyfriend. I knew the dos and don'ts of dating, but I didn't know the whys. I got pregnant in my senior year of high school. I was devastated and terrified. I had made plans to join the United States Air Force and was prepared to leave upon graduation. I met with the Air Force recruiter, and he explained that I would have to give full custody of my child to my mother to finish my enlistment. I couldn't breathe as I thought about signing my child over to my mother. So I was determined to succeed in my life in another way, even as a single mom. My boyfriend went away to college and played football as he had planned. Our child did not alter his life, but my life changed significantly.

I found a job, attended junior college, and continued to date my daughter's father. Being a single mom, attending college, and working two jobs was exhausting, so I quit college and became an apprentice at an eyewear company. I was their first and only African American employee. I loved my new job, and I enjoyed all of the people who worked with me. One day I greeted a customer who said, *"I know everybody has to hire at least one of your kind, but I will not have you waiting on me."* I said, "Not a problem, sir; let me get someone else to wait on you." I told the owner what the customer said, and she confronted him with words I cannot repeat. All of my co-workers were making sure I was all right. I assured them that I was, and I shrugged it off. But it hurt.

I continued dating my boyfriend, and I became pregnant a second time. I was embarrassed and disappointed with myself. I struggled with every negative thought possible. It seemed that the only right thing to do was marry my children's father. He had often asked me to marry him, so now might be the right time. While planning to marry my boyfriend, one of my best friends asked me a difficult question: "Are you getting married because you're pregnant?" I shrugged my shoulders like, "Maybe." She continued, "You two really don't get along very well. You shouldn't get married." I was shocked, but she was right. We broke up, and I was devastated by the broken relationship.

> **IT WAS TOUGH GROWING OUT OF MY OLD LEGALISTIC WAYS. I WAS TRYING TO PLEASE GOD BY LIVING UP TO THE LAW OF GOD BECAUSE I FELT LIKE THAT IS WHAT I OWED HIM.**

Fortunately, I turned to the church for answers, and I heard a clear presentation of the Gospel. I chose to receive Jesus as my personal Lord and Savior, and I was born again. Jesus' giving his life for me on the cross was the ultimate demonstration of His love for me and the evidence I needed that proved my value and worth. I was excited about this new commitment that I had made to Christ. However, it was tough growing out of my old legalistic ways. I was trying to please God by living up to the Law of God because I felt like that is what I owed Him. I relied on my own strength and resources instead of relying on Him. I realized that living up to the law was due to a lack of faith in God. After being involved in the church for four years, I was appointed as Youth Director. Like my church experience in California, I was part of a family.

I loved being a mother—and I had two amazing baby girls who needed me to be present in their lives—but it was not easy being a single mom. There were days when I felt utterly exhausted and overwhelmed. Doubts about my faith crept in, but I chose to cry out to the Lord and believe His plan for me was more significant than the hardships I was experiencing.

As the Youth Director, I took the students to a conference in Atlanta, where I met Daryl. He was performing with *Transformation Crusade*, a Christian hip-hop group. I was impressed with hearing this hip-hop group present a clear presentation of the Gospel. As we listened to what they had to say through their message, they challenged us to go deeper in our walk with God. Daryl asked if we could keep in touch after the conference, and I said, "Yes." While developing a relationship with Daryl all of my insecurities began to show. I had to come to grips with the fact that I didn't believe God could keep me from getting hurt again or that I could move past the shame of having two children out of wedlock.

Adding to my pain was my father, who chose not to be in our lives. He never called, wrote, or visited us while living in California. When we moved back to North Carolina, I chose to see him and establish some type of relationship. In the process, I discovered that he was not a believer in Jesus Christ. When I visited him, he was always glad to see me, and he would introduce me to his friends by saying, "Look at my daughter, isn't she the prettiest girl in the world?" I thought to myself, "You don't even know me." However, I wasn't completely devoid of a father figure in my life. The pastor in California at New Pleasant Hill Missionary Baptist Church, Rev. Melvin Hill and his wife Ola Hill still refer to me as their daughter. He and his entire family have remained close to me after all these years.

When Daryl and I got married, I invited my dad to the wedding, but I told him he would not be giving me away because he hadn't taken the time to get to know the man I was marrying, nor did he have a relationship with me. When he didn't show up at my wedding, I wasn't surprised. I forgave him and continued to pursue a relationship with him. I am so thankful I did because Daryl led my father to the Lord before he died.

MOVING ON TOGETHER

We were married after two and a half years of dating, and we moved into the beautiful house Stephanie had purchased. Stephanie had worked for seven years as an optician and continued to do so until we moved to Nashville, TN–Music City, USA. Daryl and Chris had a record deal with Benson Records. My (Daryl's) degree was in psychology. I found employment in the Department of Human Services, and Stephanie found work as an optician.

We both had a good deal of unresolved spiritual, mental, and emotional baggage from our pasts and quickly discovered that marriage doesn't resolve those issues; it exposes them. From the outside, it may have appeared that we were thriving as a couple. We were attending church, had daily devotions, and were involved with a community of believers, but we were struggling. In fact, we were barely surviving the attacks from the enemy, and we were both convinced that the other person was the problem.

At the peak of our difficulties, we were invited to a Freedom in Christ conference at Christ Presbyterian Church in Brentwood, Tennessee. We both started the conference hoping the other person would be fixed, but we both realized the speaker was talking to us as individuals. During the conference, Dr. Anderson said, "No one can keep you from being the person God created you to be, but yourself." We both ended up in tears as he shared these words, "as believers in Christ, God is our heavenly Father, and we are his children whom He dearly loves." Then he

> EXPERIENCING SPIRITUAL FREEDOM DOESN'T MEAN BEING SPIRITUALLY MATURE. RESOLVING PERSONAL AND SPIRITUAL CONFLICTS IS A BEGINNING, NOT AN END.

explained the battle for our minds and the emotional healing that comes from forgiving those who have hurt us. Daryl was significantly helped when Neil explained why people are sharply awakened at 3 a.m. and what to do about it. It was a relief to realize I was not crazy, and others were experiencing similar attacks from the enemy.

At the end of the conference, we were led through *The Steps to Freedom in Christ*[1]. It was an encounter with God that forever changed our lives. We wept as we forgave those whom we believed had hurt us and those who rejected us for the color of our skin. We confessed our sexual sins and gave our bodies to God as living sacrifices. We forgave our parents, who did not completely understand how to provide the spiritual covering we needed, nor did they know how to teach us to fight the battle against the enemy through our personal relationship with Christ. We acknowledged our pride and rebellion. We confessed and forsook the generational sins. When we were done, Neil asked us to close our eyes and be still. Then he asked if our minds were quiet and if we sensed the peace of God that passes all understanding. We could hardly believe it. Never had we known such peace, and we knew we were free in Christ. Free from our past and free from the bondage of sin.

> **REPENTANCE INCLUDES REPLACING THE LIES I HAVE BELIEVED WITH THE TRUTH OF GOD'S WORD.**

We were cautioned that getting free and staying free are two different issues. Genuine repentance removes the barriers to our intimacy with God but experiencing spiritual freedom doesn't mean being spiritually mature. Resolving personal and spiritual conflicts is a beginning, not an end. Now we were free to grow, but there were still some issues that we needed to work through before being able to help others.

STEPHANIE'S TAKEAWAYS

It takes a while to process your new life, freedom and identity in Christ. I knew there would be challenges ahead, but I really believed I could face them as a child of God.

Even when Daryl and I are not walking in agreement, I choose to believe who we both are in Christ. In time we have grown to love each other as Christ loves the church. Daryl happily took on the responsibility of raising my first two children. We also encouraged them to maintain a relationship with their biological father, which they have. They later had the privilege of seeing their biological father come to Christ. Ashley works as a client service manager with a financial firm, and Shayna is on staff at their church in Tampa, Fla. We went on to have three more children together. They are now adults and part of a music group called *The New Respects*. They share the love of God through pop, soul, and rock & roll!

A big takeaway for me was realizing how the past has a hold on us but how that is overcome when we become new creations in Christ and truly forgive those who have offended us. I have often said, "I forgive you," but, in hindsight, I had not. A dear friend once told me, "When the situation is small, and your response is huge, there is a problem." When I was a single mom occasionally my girls had to go home alone directly after school instead of going to their grandmother's house. I asked them to call me when they arrived home so that I would know they had arrived safely.

One day while working with a client, I looked at my watch, and I thought, "Hmm…they should have called by now." I called home and asked, "Why didn't you call me?" They said, "We called you, but your boss said you were with a client." I asked, "Is everything okay?" They said, "Yes!" I hung up the phone and immediately confronted my boss. I said, "Why didn't you ask me to come to the phone when my girls called? I told you they would be home alone today, and whenever they call, you should always ask me to come to the phone!" My boss, who was like family, knew and loved my girls and was shocked by my tone. He said, "I'm sorry," with a puzzled look on his face. Now I realize that my response was not just about my girls but also my past. As a child growing up in California, there were times when I did not feel safe due to the environment I was living in. A current event triggered my past insecurities. Fortunately, at the time my boss was compassionate and forgave me. Now I see how current events can trigger wounds from our past, and wounds that aren't healed are transferred to others.

DARYL'S TAKEAWAYS

My college roommate and rap partner, Chris Williamson, was recruited by a Presbyterian church to begin a new multiracial congregation. Chris was a gifted communicator, and the church grew rapidly. He invited me to join his staff as the Youth Pastor. My role eventually evolved into becoming the Family Pastor. To help me with my new position, I selected every book I could find of Dr. Anderson's to purchase at the local Christian bookstore. As I walked up to the counter, I had so many of Neil's books, the lady at the counter started a conversation with me and asked if I would like to meet him. I was surprised to hear he lived in Franklin, Tennessee because I thought he lived in California, where the Freedom In Christ office was once located, but I gladly gave her my contact information. I was excited to meet him because his conference made such a significant impact on our lives.

Dr. Anderson called the next day. We met and became golfing buddies, but it was a time of discipleship for me. I had gained so much spiritual knowledge from the Freedom In Christ conference and his material, but I hadn't taken the initiative to lead others through *The Steps*. I would use Freedom in Christ Ministries' material to teach, but I had never set up any personal freedom appointments. After meeting and talking to him, I asked him if he would do a conference at our church, and he agreed.

During the conference, a lady asked if she could have a personal session with Neil, and he offered it to her if she would allow me to sit in as a prayer partner. So, we met the following Monday. Neil listened to her story and asked if she would like to resolve the issues she brought up. She said she would, and with her permission, Neil began leading her through *The Steps*. In one of the Steps, she prayed and asked God to reveal to her mind who she needed to forgive. Neil sat with a tablet and wrote down the names that came to her mind. The third person she mentioned was me.

After she had processed that Step, she said she needed a break. When she left the room Neil looked at me and said, "I think you know what you need to do." I said, "I do," and when she returned, I asked her to forgive me for avoiding her, which I had done because I didn't know what to do to help her. That was a significant turning point in my life and gave me the courage to help others as I had been helped. The first opportunity came from our own church staff. Our Children's Director struggled with fear and night terrors and was asking for prayer from the church staff. I've learned that praying for someone without helping them deal with the root causes of their problem is not very effective. What is effective is their prayer and repentance. I offered to lead her through *The Steps*, and she sent the following testimony to Dr. Anderson:

> I thought my story was unique, but I often wondered if anyone else had the spiritual conflicts I was suffering with. My problem began a couple of years ago. I was experiencing demonic nightmares and had nights in which I felt the presence of something or someone in my room. One night I woke up feeling like someone was choking me, and I could not speak or say the name of Jesus. I was terrified. I sought

help from church leaders and pastors. They had no idea how to encourage me. Eventually, fear turned into a panic anxiety disorder, and my thoughts were so loud, destructive, and frightening that I visited my primary care provider. I thought she would understand my belief that this was a spiritual battle. When I expressed the idea that the enemy was attacking me, she responded by diagnosing me with bipolar disorder and told me that I would be on medication for the rest of my life. She also gave me a prescription for anti-depressants and anti-anxiety meds. I was devastated.

I told my husband the diagnosis, and he assured me that it wasn't true. I decided not to take the medication. I just didn't have any peace about it. My pastors prayed over me, but nothing changed. I began Christian counseling, which helped a bit, but it was nowhere near worth the $400 per month that I paid. When I told my Christian counselor about what was happening in my mind and about my fears, she too said, "I think it is time for medication." It seemed like everyone thought I was crazy. No one believed that my problem was spiritual.

Thankfully, I came across one of your books and read stories of people I could relate to. I knew there was an answer. In that book, I first heard of *The Steps to Freedom In Christ*. Honestly, I was afraid of *The Steps* at first. I didn't know what to expect, but one of our pastors had recently met Dr. Anderson and learned how to lead people through *The Steps*. He offered to help me, and I accepted.

Going through *The Steps* was one of the most challenging yet incredible things I've ever done. I experienced a lot of interference, such as headaches and confusion, but having the Holy Spirit reveal to me all that I needed to renounce was incredible. When I prayed and asked God to bring my ancestors' sins to my mind, I was shocked at all that came up. I don't even know my ancestors! I later asked my mother about the things that came to my mind during the session, and she confirmed that my family had been involved in those things. I was amazed by how the Holy Spirit brought out the truth.

After going through *The Steps,* my mind was completely silent. It was amazing. There were no nagging thoughts. I was totally at peace. I wanted to cry with joy. After that, I wasn't afraid of being alone, and the nightmares were gone. I didn't have to play the radio or television to drown out the terrible thoughts. I could sit in silence and be still.

That was my first experience leading someone through *The Steps,* and it shows it doesn't take a lot of experience to be effective. After that, I started taking many others through *The Steps* with excellent results. Every freedom appointment was a learning experience, and it also facilitated the need to work on my own issues. The presence of God is the only reason the process works, and if I haven't dealt with my own issues, they will surface in my own life as I help others.

Neil and I continued to meet and talk through these issues. I kept telling him, "You are messing with my mind. I don't know how to do church anymore." Three songs and a Sunday morning message to encourage people were good, but it was no longer cutting it for me.

I realized how people are sitting in church dealing with all types of unresolved mental and emotional conflicts and are being tormented by Satan. Those unresolved conflicts were the very issues Satan was using against them to accuse them and keep them in bondage. I could no longer sit by and watch people go to church Sunday after Sunday going through the motions, silently struggling just to make it.

TOGETHER IN MINISTRY

We met with Dr. Anderson to pursue the possibility of going on staff with Freedom in Christ Ministries. The desire was there, but the thought of raising our own support was intimidating. He suggested we start by going through the training that all staff and ministry associates have to go through. It culminates with a four day practicum where we were led through *The Steps* in a one-on-one appointment. Then we were observed leading another through *The Steps*. It was an incredible four days. We accepted the challenge and began raising our own support.

Working together is a dream come true. That could never have happened when we were first married. Just living together was a challenge. We have seen God work in people's lives in ways that we never knew were even possible. The rest of this book will share how and why this works and how it can work in your life and ministry.

CHAPTER 2

Overcoming Identity Crisis

Who are you? If someone asked you to describe your identity, how would you answer? Every person born on this planet has a natural curiosity to know who they are and why they exist. It is the most important question you and I will ever answer. When people ask who you are, you may be tempted to respond by giving your name. Our names are Daryl Fitzgerald and Stephanie (Rogers) Fitzgerald. Those are the birth names our parents gave to us when we were born, but our names are not who we are. Sometimes we try to find out who we are by identifying with our cultural heritage or race. I am African American, European, Latino, Asian, or something else. There is great value in our racial differences and our ethnic distinctiveness, but that is not who we are. Who you are and your identity is far more than your name or cultural heritage. If you try to find your identity through your race or your cultural heritage, you will be living beneath the privileges of who you really are. You also may try to find your identity by what you do. Perhaps you are a CEO of a big corporation, a professional basketball player, a football player, a golfer, or a pastor. No, that is your job, it describes what you do, but that is not who you are. What you do, the amount of money you make, or your educational attainment doesn't answer the question of who you are.

SPIRITUAL BEINGS IN A PHYSICAL BODY

As we have walked with people to help them understand who they are, we ask them to discuss the following question: **"Are you a man or woman who has a spirit, or are you a spirit in a man or woman's body?"** When God spoke to Jeremiah, He said, "Before I formed you in the womb, I knew you" (Jeremiah 1:5). How did God know Jeremiah before he was physically born? As spiritual beings created in God's image, our human spirit is made in His image. Our spirit resembles the same nature, attributes, and moral character as God. Before Jeremiah was physically born, God placed in Jeremiah's

> **IF YOU TRY TO FIND YOUR IDENTITY THROUGH YOUR RACE OR YOUR CULTURAL HERITAGE, YOU WILL BE LIVING BENEATH THE PRIVILEGES OF WHO YOU REALLY ARE.**

human spirit the gifts, talents, personality, and plan to carry out His will on the earth. God then physically knit Jeremiah together in his mother's womb (Psalms 139:13). God knew Jeremiah because God planned Jeremiah's life before he was born. Just like Jeremiah, God knows us as well. We all are spiritual beings who have been given gifts, talents, and the personality to carry out God's will on the earth. We all are spiritual beings in a physical body.

This unique combination of "dust" (body) and divine breath (spirit) constituted Adam's original nature in Genesis 1 and set him apart from the rest of creation. Like a light bulb connected to electricity, the lives of Adam and Eve reflected the life and light of God. As a "living soul," Adam was both physically and spiritually alive. He was physically alive because his soul, or spirit, was united with his physical body. He was spiritually alive because his soul was united with God.

Before the fall, Adam and Eve understood their divine purpose, which was to rule over the birds of the sky, the beasts of the field, and the fish of the sea. God intended them to rule with one another as equals, not over one another as slaves.

> **"ARE YOU A MAN OR WOMAN WHO HAS A SPIRIT, OR ARE YOU A SPIRIT IN A MAN OR WOMAN'S BODY?"**

Adam and Eve had a divine purpose. They were given a specific role as God's image-bearers to distinctly function in their given sexuality as male and female representatives on the earth. They never had to search for identity; they were given a divine identity as children of God! They didn't have to search for significance. They had complete support from the God of the universe, who walked with them in the cool of the day. They were safe and secure and had a deep sense of belonging to God and to each other. They were also naked and unashamed. They could have sexual intercourse with one another in the presence of God to reproduce and fill the earth with no sense of guilt and shame.

LOSS OF PURPOSE, MEANING, AND IDENTITY

When Adam and Eve chose to sin against God's command, they lost their life and light. They no longer reflected the life of God because they were no longer connected to Him (see John 8:12). "And the Lord God commanded the man, 'You are free to eat from any tree of the garden, but you must not eat from the tree of the knowledge of good and evil, for when you eat from it, you will certainly die'" (Genesis 2:16,17). Adam and Eve disobeyed God, and they ate from the tree. Did they die physically? Not immediately, although physical death would ultimately be a consequence. However, they did die spiritually, and the impact of spiritual death was immediate. They lost their relationship with God. They lost their identity. They no longer knew who they were! They lost their sense of purpose and meaning in life. They no longer knew why they existed! They lost trust in one another and their trust in God.

> ❝ GOD INTENDED THEM TO RULE WITH ONE ANOTHER AS EQUALS, NOT OVER ONE ANOTHER AS SLAVES. ❞

They no longer knew how to be in a relationship with God or each other! They no longer felt safe or secure. In short, every part of their being, spirit, soul, and body was plunged into darkness. They were left in a severe identity crisis!

MENTAL, EMOTIONAL, AND SPIRITUAL EFFECTS OF THE FALL

When God approached Adam, Adam tried to hide from God. How does one hide from an omnipresent God? Such a distorted concept of God is a significant part of mental illness. Adam became a natural man who could no longer discern the things of God because he was disconnected from the life of God (1 Corinthians 2:14). After the fall, Adam's first emotion was, "I was afraid" (Genesis 3:10). What was he afraid of? He had no neurological illness that required medication, no defense mechanisms that he needed to defend himself, nor any flesh patterns that had to be crucified. That primordial fear was evidence of the absence of life, and it has plagued humanity for every generation since. Anxiety disorders are one of the most common mental health disorders in the world. "Do not fear" is the most repeated commandment in Scripture, occurring around 400 times[1]. However, telling someone not to be afraid doesn't work because anxiety disorders arise out of a state of disconnection, not disobedience.

Adam was like the Gentiles who walked "in the futility of their mind, being darkened in their understanding, excluded from the life of God" (Ephesians 4:17, 18 NASB; emphasis added). Adam and Eve's innocence was replaced by guilt and shame. Their offspring struggled with depression and anger. Cain brought a grain offering to God, who was not pleased: "Cain became very angry, and his countenance fell. Then the Lord said to Cain, 'Why are you angry, and why has your countenance fallen? If you do well, will not your countenance be lifted up? And if you do not do well, sin is crouching at the door, and its desire is for you, but you must master it" (Genesis 4:5-7 NASB).

The Hebrew word for 'crouching' (*shachach*) is the same as an ancient Babylonian word referring to an evil demon crouching at the door of a building to threaten the people inside.[1] What was the cause of their mental and emotional depravity and sinful behavior? There was no pollution of any kind in their environment, and they couldn't blame mom and dad. Only one thing changed in their experience: They died spiritually! They were separated from God, the source of life! If you believe the Bible and God's Word, there is only one overarching answer for the mental, emotional, physical, and spiritual problems that plague the world and the Church today. The entire human race desperately needs to be reconciled to God (see John 3:16).

A LOST UNDERSTANDING OF OUR VALUE AND TRUE IDENTITY

After the fall, every descendant of Adam was born physically alive but spiritually dead. We all are born into this world at a spiritual disadvantage because we are born in sin and shaped in iniquity (Psalm

51:5). We enter into this world facing spiritual, mental, emotional, and physical challenges because we all have lost our identity and a true sense of who we are.

Deep within our spirit, there is a longing and a desire to find our identity, purpose, and meaning in life. As a result, we set out on a journey to find our value. We seek significance and value through the approval of others and through our cultural heritage, education, or financial status. All of our efforts, as well-intended as they are, will not fill the space in our heart outside of Jesus. Our identity, sense of purpose, and meaning in life come from being reconciled to God and understanding our identity as his children.

BECOMING SLAVES OF SATAN

The fall had another disastrous result. Through lies and deception, Adam and Eve lost their dominion to rule the earth. The power and authority to rule over the earth was handed over to Satan. He now has total control to rule the kingdoms of the world (Matthew 4:8). Jesus referred to Satan as the "ruler of this world" (John 12:31, 16:11). Paul calls him the "prince of the power of the air" and "the god of this world" (2 Corinthians 4:4) and instructed believers to put on the armor of God. "For our struggle is not against flesh and blood, but against the rulers, against the authorities, against the powers of this dark world and against the spiritual forces of evil in the heavenly realms" (Ephesians 6: 12). "As for you, you were dead your transgressions and sins, in which you used to live when you followed the ways of this world and of the ruler of the kingdom of the air, the spirit who is now at work in those who are disobedient" (Ephesians 2:1,2). Our loss of dominion over the earth was Satan's gain. We are all subject to becoming his slaves through temptation, accusations, lies, and deception.

Although I (Daryl) was taught to go to church every Sunday and Wednesday, I did not have a clear understanding of how to fight against the enemy. As a result, I became a slave to Satan's schemes that produced a lot of fear and ungodly beliefs in my life. Thank God for the truth! The Bible never says we should fear Satan, but it does teach that the fear of God is the beginning of wisdom. I remember hearing in church that Jesus has all power over the enemy, but the conversations in the church about demons or Satan were based on fear. I remember singing that Jesus is the answer for the world today, but I could not find the solutions I encountered for the spiritual warfare I experienced. Consider the irony: The African American Church provided hope during the days of physical slavery, but I could not find the answers in the

> **THE AFRICAN AMERICAN CHURCH PROVIDED HOPE DURING THE DAYS OF PHYSICAL SLAVERY, BUT I COULD NOT FIND THE ANSWERS IN THE CHURCH TO ADDRESS SPIRITUAL SLAVERY.**

Church to address spiritual slavery. Clearly, my ancestors and I had very different experiences at Church.

My lack of knowledge of the truth made me spiritually vulnerable to Satan's schemes. In my spirit, I somehow knew that Jesus was the answer to my problems, but I didn't understand how He could help me. I never understood the power of the Gospel or the essence of what it meant to be a child of God. Going to church, I often felt that being a saint was something I could never attain. I felt like I could do everything right but still not be a saint. I fell victim to Satan's lies, and that was tormenting! Paul wrote, concerning the times we live in today, "The Spirit clearly says that in later times some will abandon the faith and follow deceiving spirits and things taught by demons" (1 Timothy 4:1). Would you want your schoolteacher or university professor to be Satan or a demon teaching your child in the classroom? Anyone in their right mind would say no. We have found that people worldwide are being enslaved to Satan by paying attention to deceiving spirits and believing the lies of the enemy. John wrote, "The whole world is under the control of the evil one" (1 John 5:19).

> **GOING TO CHURCH, I OFTEN FELT THAT BEING A SAINT WAS SOMETHING I COULD NEVER ATTAIN. I FELT LIKE I COULD DO EVERYTHING RIGHT BUT STILL NOT BE A SAINT.**

The decisions made by Adam and Eve produced a real mess! To try to make the best out of a bad situation, God raised up Moses to deliver the Israelites from Egypt and gave them the Law, but they couldn't keep it. God sent prophets to correct the people, but they were stoned or largely ignored. The wise, rich, and politically powerful Solomon tried to find purpose and meaning in life independently of God and concluded, "Meaningless, meaningless! All is meaningless" (Ecclesiastes 1:2). Who has the answers for the woes of this fallen world and humanity? We believe the Church does. A. B. Bruce wrote in *The Training of the Twelve*[2], "Jesus was inaugurating a process of spiritual emancipation which was to issue in the complete deliverance of the apostles, and through them of the Christian church."

JESUS, THE SECOND ADAM (RESTORED IDENTITY)

What Adam and Eve lost in the Garden of Eden was spiritual life. Jesus' purpose for coming to earth was to restore the spiritual life that was lost in the Garden (see Genesis 2:17), destroy Satan's works (see 1 John 3:8), and restore us to our rightful position of power, authority, and relationship with God as his children. Like the first Adam, Jesus was both physically and spiritually alive. His entire life was an example for us to follow. Being fully God and fully man, He developed as a man, and He "grew in wisdom [mental] and stature [physical], and in favor with God [spiritual] and man [social]" (Luke 2:52). Jesus was tempted in every way to live his life independent of God, just like Adam and Eve, yet did not sin. All temptation attempts to entice us to live our lives independently of God. Jesus, however, demonstrated total reliance upon God the Father and resisted the lies of the devil (see Matthew 4:1-11). In doing so, He showed us how a spiritually alive person has the power to overcome the lies of the enemy and live a righteous life.

Helping people to be reconciled to God is not building our natural lives into each other. It is helping people grow and understand who they are "in Christ" so they become firmly rooted "in Christ" (Colossians 2:7). This is the essence of true discipleship. Making disciples is not about building people up to be like us. It is not found in self-determination, strengthening your self-esteem, or attempting to succeed in your natural strength. It is about teaching people to follow Jesus. In Him is where you are being built up to know who you are and find purpose and meaning in life.

MAKING BIBLICAL DISCIPLES

Jesus didn't confront the disciples right away with their need to control their natural lives in order to gain eternal life. Instead, He invited them to follow Him. He demonstrated His authority over nature, illnesses, and demons. When He thought they were ready, Jesus called the twelve together and "gave them power and authority to drive out all demons and to cure diseases, and he sent them out to proclaim the kingdom of God and to heal the sick" (Luke 9:1-2). Jesus told them they could not take anything with them on their journey because He wanted them to be totally dependent upon Him. Jesus used this opportunity to share a central theme for all four gospels and the core basis for making reproducible disciples. "Whoever wants to be my disciple must deny themselves, take up their cross daily and follow me. For whoever wants to save their life will lose it, but whoever loses their life for me will save it. What good is it for someone to gain the whole world, and yet lose or forfeit their very self" (Luke 9:23-25)? Those who seek to find their identity, purpose, and the meaning of life in their natural existence will never find it. Relying on your own strength to find life is how you lose it. Depending on Christ's strength is how you find it.

> **" THOSE WHO SEEK TO FIND THEIR IDENTITY, PURPOSE, AND THE MEANING OF LIFE IN THEIR NATURAL EXISTENCE WILL NEVER FIND IT. RELYING ON YOUR OWN STRENGTH TO FIND LIFE IS HOW YOU LOSE IT. DEPENDING ON CHRIST'S STRENGTH IS HOW YOU FIND IT. "**

KINGDOMS IN CONFLICT

The Lord appointed seventy-two others and sent them out, but they came back with a different report than the twelve did. "The seventy-two returned with joy and said, 'Lord, even the demons submit to us in your name'" (Luke 10:17). Jesus said, "I saw Satan fall like lightning from heaven. I have given you authority to trample on snakes and scorpions and to overcome the power of the enemy; nothing will harm you. However, do not rejoice that the spirits submit to you, but rejoice that your names are written in heaven" (verses 19,20). That is an essential lesson for servant leaders. Don't rejoice that you have power and authority over the enemy but rejoice that you are a child of God. As his children you have been given the right to rule. The last thing the devil wants you to know is who you are in Christ. Jesus encourages us to focus on the answer, not the problem. All the analysis in the world doesn't set anyone free.

> ❝ THE LAST THING THE DEVIL WANTS YOU TO KNOW IS WHO YOU ARE IN CHRIST. ❞

When you became a Christian, you were transferred from the kingdom of darkness to the Kingdom of Heaven. "For he has rescued us from the dominion of darkness and brought us into the kingdom of the Son he loves" (Col. 1:13). "For our citizenship is in heaven, from which also we eagerly wait for a Savior, the Lord Jesus Christ" (Phil. 3:20, NASB). While it is true that we have to obey the laws of this country, we have been transferred into a spiritual kingdom, and our King is the Lord Jesus Christ. Our identity is in him. The Kingdom of Heaven is a spiritual and eternal kingdom invisible to the physical eye. God desires us to look at ourselves through the eyes of the spirit, not through the eyes of our experience. We live in His kingdom by faith, not by sight. Jesus said that we can't point out this kingdom to anyone.

> ❝ GOD DESIRES US TO LOOK AT OURSELVES THROUGH THE EYES OF THE SPIRIT, NOT THROUGH THE EYES OF OUR EXPERIENCE. ❞

"Nor will they say, 'Look, here it is!' or 'There it is!'" Yet He also said that the kingdom is very real. "For behold, the kingdom of God is in your midst" (Luke 17:21, NASB). The power available to us is the same power that raised Christ from the dead. The apostle Paul prayed that we might perceive "the surpassing greatness of His power toward us who believe. These are in accordance with the working of the strength of His might which He brought about in Christ when He raised Him from the dead and seated Him at His right hand in the heavenly places" (Eph. 1:19,20, NASB).

The Bible portrays a battle between two kingdoms, between true prophets and false prophets, between the Spirit of truth and the father of lies, and between Christ and the antichrist. Discipleship is kingdom building, and the kingdom of darkness is the opposition. Adam and Eve forfeited their right to rule, and Satan became the rebel ruler and authority over the earth. After the resurrection, Jesus said, "All authority in heaven and on earth has been given to me. Therefore, go and make disciples of all the nations, baptizing them in the name of the Father, and of the Son and of the Holy Spirit" (Matthew 28:18,19). Who has the right to rule is the primary question when there are two kingdoms in conflict.

IN CHRIST WE HAVE AUTHORITY AND POWER

Jesus never appealed to His authority as the basis for what He did and spoke, and yet, "He taught as one having authority, and not as their scribes" (Matthew 7:29). However, He did refer to His authority in giving the Great Commission because one cannot delegate responsibility without authority. Authority and power were initially offered only to the twelve and the seventy, but that would change after Pentecost. The disciples were told to wait in Jerusalem until they received power when the Holy Spirit would come upon them (Acts 1:8). Only then could they be effective witnesses because the resurrected life of Christ would be within them. Pentecost was the beginning of the Church, and now every born-again believer has the authority and power to do God's will. Power is the ability to rule, and authority is the right to rule. Every true believer who is dependent upon God has both because of who they are in Christ. Our ability to make disciples is based on our identity and position in Christ, which the apostle Paul explains in Ephesians 1:1-2,10. He starts by explaining our inheritance in Christ and prays, "That the eyes of your heart may be enlightened so that you will know what is the hope of his calling, what are the riches of the glory of his inheritance in the saints, and what is the surpassing greatness of his power toward us who believe. These are in accordance with the working of the strength of his might which he brought about in Christ when he raised him from the dead and seated him at his right hand in the heavenly places, far above all rule and authority and power and dominion" (Ephesians 1:18-20 NASB). We are also seated with Christ in the "heavenly places" (2:6), which is the spiritual realm. Because of our position in Christ, we have the authority to do His will; and when we are filled with His Spirit, we have the power. Therefore, "Be strong in the Lord and in the strength of his might" (Ephesians 6:10). It is His authority and His power, but we have "become partakers of the divine nature" (2 Peter 1:4) because our souls are in union with God.

REPENTANCE: THE KEY TO RESOLVING PERSONAL & SPIRITUAL CONFLICTS

We have observed two significant deficiencies in many churches. The first is a lack of genuine repentance. Jesus said, "The time is fulfilled, and the kingdom of God is at hand; repent and believe the gospel" (Mark 1:15). Repentance is not merely a change of behavior. It is a change of thinking. People come to church carrying a lot of baggage from their past. They hear a good message, sing some songs, pick up their baggage, and take it back home with them! It is because they don't change their mind. They don't change how they think about the baggage. The message made them feel good, but that is as far as it goes. There are many opportunities for Christians to be educated in their faith, but very few opportunities exist to repent, and in most cases, we are not sure how. When Stephanie and I were first called into ministry, we didn't know how to help people resolve their mental, emotional, and spiritual conflicts. We didn't even know how to resolve our own personal and spiritual conflicts.

Let me give an example. Stephanie and I walked with a young man who was a dedicated Christian. He served in a Christian ministry and was full of life, but he had struggled with sexual feelings toward other men and acted on those feelings on a few occasions. He tried everything he knew to get free, but he couldn't get over the fact that he had these feelings. Since he struggled in his thought life so badly, he felt emotionally struck. He resigned himself to believe the lie that he would struggle with same-sex attraction for the rest of his life, which is not entirely true. However, if he continued to mentally entertain the fantasies in his mind about same-sex relationships and give himself over to those images, Satan would provide the opportunity for those urges to be acted upon. Instead he could choose to take the time to understand the truth of who God created him to be as a child of God, learn to take the responsibility to take thoughts captive and transform his mind, and choose to walk according to the Spirit and not entertain the desires of his flesh. He

> **FEELINGS ARE A PRODUCT OF WHAT YOU ARE THINKING, BUT FEELINGS DO NOT NECESSARILY REFLECT WHAT IS TRUE. BELIEVING A LIE DOES NOT MEAN IT IS TRUE, AND NOT BELIEVING THE TRUTH DOES NOT MEAN IT IS A LIE.**

would not have to resign himself to believe he had to struggle with the same old flesh patterns. With time and effort he could then break the cycle of those mental strongholds and have the real possibility of walking in the freedom that was purchased for him in Christ. The emotions and urges that this young man was feeling were real. However, feelings are a product of what you are thinking, but feelings do not necessarily reflect what is true. Believing a lie does not mean it is accurate, and not believing the truth does not mean it is a lie. Jesus died for all of our sins to set us free, but Satan will remind us of our sins to keep us in bondage. This young man's struggle with sin was taken care of at the cross.

> **❝ BEING TEMPTED, ACCUSED, AND LIED TO BY SATAN DOES NOT SHOW THAT SIN CONTROLS OUR LIVES. IT SHOWS THAT SATAN USES TEMPTATION, ACCUSATION, AND DECEPTION TO GET US TO LIVE OUR LIVES INDEPENDENT OF GOD'S MORAL STANDARD SO HE CAN GAIN CONTROL OVER OUR LIVES. ❞**

However, because of his past experience with sin, he created a pattern of thinking that eventually formed into a conduct of behavior. To fight against those strongholds, his job was to repent (change his thoughts) and walk in the truth of God's Word. With time and effort, his emotions would line up with the truth. Dealing with the sin of same-sex attraction is no different than dealing with the sin of pornography or adultery. We must deal with the process of renewing our minds to daily fight against the temptation, accusation, and deception from Satan. Being tempted, accused, and lied to by Satan does not show that sin controls our lives. It shows that Satan uses temptation, accusation, and deception to get us to live our lives independent of God's moral standard so he can gain control over our lives. Satan waits for those opportunities to do so, but Jesus came to destroy the works of the devil (1 John 3:8).

"And do not give the devil an opportunity to lead you into sin by holding a grudge, or nurturing anger, or harboring resentment, or cultivating bitterness" (see Ephesians 4:27 AMP). Going through the repentance process in *The Steps to Freedom,* God revealed to this young man that he had deep emotional wounds from never feeling loved or supported by his father. It left him completely emotionally vulnerable to Satan's attacks, and Satan took full advantage of those vulnerable emotions.

People are encouraged to confess their sins, but they are likely to be trapped in the sin, confess, sin, confess, and sin again cycle if that is all they are doing. Confession is only the first step toward repentance. Repentance and faith in God are the only effective and lasting means by which we can resolve personal and spiritual conflicts. If that is a new concept for you, please give us a chance to explain what we have learned about conflict resolution based solely on the Word of God.

THE WHOLE GOSPEL

The second deficiency is an incomplete Gospel. Most believers are laboring under only part of the Gospel. They believe that Jesus is the Messiah who came to die for their sins, and that, hopefully, Heaven awaits them when they die if they put their trust in God. That is partially true, but that would leave them believing that eternal life is something they get when they die, which is not true. "And the testimony is this, that God has given us eternal life, and this life is in his Son. He who has the Son has the life; he who does not have the Son of God does not have the life" (1 John 5:11,12). The early

Church defined salvation as union with God. Union with God is most often communicated in the epistles as being "in Christ" or "in Him." There are forty such prepositional phrases in the book of Ephesians alone. What Adam and Eve lost in the fall was life, and that is what Jesus came to give us (John 10:10). He also came to destroy the works of the devil (1 John 3:8). Because of who we are in Christ, we have power and authority over darkness and the works of Satan. That is the Gospel we are waiting to hear, and it is just as much a part of the Gospel as is our forgiveness and new life in Christ. Paul summarizes the whole Gospel in Colossians 2:13-15:

> When you were dead in your transgressions and the uncircumcision of your flesh, He made you alive together with him, having forgiven us all our transgressions, having canceled the certificate of debt consisting of decrees against us, which was hostile to us; and he has taken it out of the way, having nailed it to the cross. When he disarmed the rulers and authorities, he made a public display of them, having triumphed over them through him.

Let us give you a sobering thought: Believing the Gospel means you have been born of God, you are a new creation, and your citizenship is in Heaven. Without believing the Gospel, you have not been born of God, you are not a child of God, and you are not a citizen of Heaven. You will live your life separated from God in hell, not because God wants you there, but because you did not choose to believe the Gospel and partake of the new life in Christ that he provided for you! "Test yourselves to see if you are in the faith; examine yourselves! Or do you not recognize this about yourselves, that Jesus Christ is in you—unless indeed you fail the test" (2 Corinthians 13:5)? Many believers have not fully incorporated the whole Gospel into their lives. We certainly hadn't. I (Daryl) had been in ministry for fifteen years before the truth of who I am in Christ fully sunk in. It was like scales fell from my eyes. Watchman Nee wrote about his experience of discovering his identity and position in Christ. He cried tears of joy when he realized that he was already alive in Christ and didn't need to strive any more to become someone he already was.[3] We are not describing a second work of grace. Being alive and free in Christ is the birthright of every child of God (see John 1:12-13). This is a foundational truth to our relationship with Christ.

The truth can't set you free if you don't know it, which is part of the problem, but lack of repentance is the more significant issue. We have quoted passages like Galatians 2:20 to hurting souls, and the impact was minimal. However, when we helped them resolve their personal and spiritual conflicts through genuine repentance and faith in God, the Scriptures came alive for them. Repentance removes sin barriers to their intimacy with God. Many who come to see us have said, "How come I couldn't see this before? Now when I read the epistles, I see repeatedly that I'm in Christ!"

FREEDOM FOR EVERY TONGUE, TRIBE, AND NATION

A young African American couple came to our office to see us. The young man was unfaithful to his wife. They both wanted to be reconciled, but his act of unfaithfulness devastated their marriage. She tried to move forward but found it hard to trust him. After going through *Victory Over the Darkness* and helping them get a clear understanding of their identity in Christ, they both recognized how much unresolved emotional, mental, and spiritual bondage they were carrying. The young man had no relationship with his father. Any communication with him was short and emotionally distant. Therefore, his relationship with God was the same as his father. He struggled to understand how much God loved him since his earthly father left the family when he was a young boy. After walking through the steps of forgiveness, he realized for the first time that God's love for him was not the same as his earthly father's love for him. He realized that God's love for him was consistent and that he was indeed a loving Father. He cried with joy when he understood that he was a child of God. His wife also gained a better understanding of her identity, and as a result, they both determined to work on themselves to build a stronger marriage.

A Spanish pastor and his wife came to our office depressed and broken. They were brought in from California by a local church to help start a church for the growing Spanish-speaking community. Within a few months, they lost their job. The husband lost all passion and zeal for ministry and wanted to quit. Taking the time to meet with us and reading *Victory Over the Darkness* brought tremendous learning and growth time for him. He said *Victory Over the Darkness* was beneficial because he had tried to find too much of his identity in what he did as a pastor and not enough on who he is in Christ. Today, he has his own church building and is excited to take the message of freedom in Christ to the Spanish community he pastors.

A struggling mother of three children was on the verge of a nervous breakdown when she asked to meet with us. After helping her resolve her personal and spiritual conflicts and instructing her about her identity and position in Christ, she sent us the following letter:

I remember being taught that I was a child of God and that the Lord loved me, but I really didn't understand what it meant. I now understand the truth behind the words I had always accepted and thought I understood. Knowing and understanding who I am in Christ opened my eyes to the truth behind words I had always heard. It was incredible, dare I say, life-changing! It freed me. Concepts in my head and words that I thought I understood changed in my mind as I discovered the truth of who I am. Thank you, Stephanie and Daryl, for showing me who I am in Christ. The truth is: I am a child of God, I am God's friend, I am justified... I was SET FREE! Before I understood the truth, I faced a tremendous amount of fear, hurt, and violation of my mind, body, and soul. I was sexually assaulted by a close family relative and thought I had forgiven that person until I was asked to pray. It felt like I hit a wall, like a load of bricks fell on top of my head. After I took a deep breath and forgave the individual and asked God to bless them, it was as if I were transformed! I was truly set free from the ugly shame and the hurt that had held on to me for so long! I was set free!

Many people who have experienced rejection, abandonment, or abuse in their early childhood have learned to believe lies like "I am not valuable," "I don't measure up," or "I am unlovable." Without exception, all of those we have discipled had unbiblical beliefs about themselves and God. My wife and I are no exception to this because we are all subject to believing such lies. When people come to us for help, we encourage them to get God's perspective of who they are instead of believing lies they may have learned through their early childhood experiences. My wife and I practice speaking over one another who God says we are and what it means, and it literally transforms how we see one another. For example, I may say to my wife, "Stephanie, you are God's child; you have the same Spirit that raised Christ from the grave living on the inside of you. Your heavenly Father created the entire universe. You belong to the King of kings and the Lord of lords!" It changes the atmosphere and the way we view one another! It proves effective when it is done consistently and over a period of time. When people come to our office, this is one of the exercises we have them practice. We encourage them to involve their entire being: spirit, soul, and body. We ask them to face one another and make eye contact. We tell them to hold hands and intentionally be mentally and emotionally present. Finally, we ask them to begin to speak God's Word of who they are "in Christ" over one another and explain what it means. We have witnessed the wonderful counselor and the Holy Spirit soften the hearts of men and women. It is beautiful to hear husbands speak the Word of God over their wives and wives speak the Word over their husbands. It is just as impactful to hear single men and women speak God's Word over themselves. We have seen tears flow from the eyes of husbands, wives, and single individuals when they begin to speak and agree with the life-giving Word of God.

Below is a list of the scriptures that describe who you are as a child of God. You don't have to work to make them true. All you have to do is believe what is true of you because this is who you are by spiritual birth. We have given the following list by way of a bookmark to thousands of struggling Christians. Some read it in disbelief, while most receive it with great joy and relief. One person said, "I didn't know God loved me that much."

IN CHRIST[5]

I am Accepted:

> JOHN 1:12—I am a child of God.

> JOHN 15:15—I am Jesus' friend.

> ROMANS 5:1—I have been accepted (justified) by God.

> 1 CORINTHIANS 6:17—I am united with the Lord and one with Him in spirit.

> 1 CORINTHIANS 6:20—I have been bought with a price; I belong to God.

> I CORINTHIANS 12:27—I am a member of Christ's body, part of His family.

> EPHESIANS 1:1—I am a saint.

> EPHESIANS 1:5—I have been adopted as God's child.

> EPHESIANS 2:18—I have direct access to God through the Holy Spirit.

> COLOSSIANS 1:14—I have been bought back (redeemed) and forgiven of all my sins.

> COLOSSIANS 2:10—I am complete in Christ.

I am Secure:

> ROMANS 8:1,2—I am free from punishment (condemnation).

> ROMANS 8:28—I am assured that all things work together for good.

> ROMANS 8:31—I am free from any condemning charges against me.

ROMANS 8:35—I cannot be separated from the love of God.

2 CORINTHIANS 1:21—I have been established, anointed, and sealed by God.

COLOSSIANS 3:3—I have died, and my life is hidden with Christ in God.

PHILIPPIANS 1:6—I am sure that the good work that God has begun in me will be finished.

PHILIPPIANS 3:20—I am a citizen of Heaven.

TIMOTHY 1:7—I have not been given a spirit of fear but of power, love, and a sound mind.

HEBREWS 4:16—I can find grace and mercy in time of need.

1 JOHN 5:18—I am born of God and the evil one cannot touch me.

I am Significant:

MATTHEW 5:13—I am the salt of the earth and light of the world.

JOHN 15:1,5—I am a part of the true vine joined to Christ and able to produce much fruit.

JOHN 15:16—I have been chosen by Jesus to bear fruit.

ACTS 1:8—I am a personal witness of Christ's.

1 CORINTHIANS 3:16—I am a temple of God.

2 CORINTHIANS 5:17—I am at peace with God and a minister of reconciliation.

2 CORINTHIANS 6:1—I am God's co-worker.

EPHESIANS 2:6—I am seated with Christ in the heavenly places.

EPHESIANS 2:10—I am God's workmanship.

EPHESIANS 3:12—I may approach God with freedom and confidence.

PHILIPPIANS 4:13—I can do all things through Christ who strengthens me.

CHAPTER 3

Overcoming the Battle for the Mind

Years ago, before getting a clear understanding of our identity in Christ, people always assumed that Stephanie and I would lead a church. On many occasions, we would be asked, "When are you starting your church?" or "We can't wait for you and Stephanie to start your church." We were constantly told that we had the "right" mentality and love to make a great pastor and first lady. It was a great compliment to both of us. However, most people did not realize that although I had no problem being a Youth and Family Pastor, I did not feel adequate to be a Senior Pastor or lead a church. I believed that Jesus died for my sins, that I was a new creation in Christ, but I still had this underlying belief that I wasn't good enough. In the back of my mind, I still thought my relationship with God was based on my performance. Much like I felt before I became a believer, I did not understand that I did not have to work *for my salvation,* but I had to work *out my salvation* (see Philippians 2:12). I believed that if I performed well enough, my relationship with God would be secure, but if I missed going to church, praying, or studying the Bible, I would have "messed up." As a result, I felt totally insecure about my salvation and relationship with God. I did not understand that attending church or doing church-related activities does not make you a child of God. What makes you a child of God is believing in the finished work of Christ. However, attending church, reading your Bible, and praying does play a part in enriching your relationship and walking with God as his child (see Hebrews 10:25). If I am honest, there are still times in my walk with Christ that I don't feel like a child of God, but my faith in God is settled even when my feelings are scattered.

> " IF I AM HONEST, THERE ARE STILL TIMES THAT I DON'T FEEL LIKE A CHILD OF GOD, BUT MY FAITH IN GOD IS SETTLED EVEN WHEN MY FEELINGS ARE SCATTERED. "

If I am a new creation in Christ, why do I struggle with the same old issues as before becoming a Christian? Why did I still feel "inadequate" or "not good enough" when people asked my wife and I when we would start a church? Why do most Christians still struggle with sin? Wouldn't it be great if when you became a new creation in Christ you did not have to deal with those feelings any longer? Unfortunately, becoming a child of God does not change your mind. Here's why it is so difficult.

SPIRIT, SOUL, AND BODY

As human beings, we are made spirit, soul, and body (see 1 Thessalonians 5:23). There is a distinct difference between the human spirit, the human soul, and the human body. However, God designed all three to function together to produce human life. The moment a person gives their life to Christ, a spiritual birth occurs. Our human spirit is totally made new! In other words, it has been made perfect because it has been born of God (see John 1:12-13). Hebrews 10:14 says, "For by one offering **he has perfected** forever those who are being sanctified." Spiritually speaking, my spirit is in the same condition Adam & Eve's spirits were before they fell in the Garden of Eden. What about the soul and body? Unfortunately, they are still a work in progress. They have not yet been perfected. They are still under construction! Our bodies, mind, will, emotions, memories, thoughts, and habits still need to undergo a complete transformation. That is why we still struggle with the same old issues. If my body was new, why would God have to one day transform our lowly bodies so that they will be like his glorious body (see Philippians 3:21)? Why do our bodies grow weary and long to put on our heavenly bodies like new clothes (see 2 Corinthians 5:2)? If my mind has been made new, why would it need to be transformed (see Romans 12:2)? Why do I have to set my mind on things above (Colossians 3:2)? We have learned to live our lives separated from God for so long that our minds have been conditioned to live independently of him. We

BECOMING A CHILD OF GOD DOES NOT CHANGE YOUR MIND.

must now learn how to reverse these flesh patterns by depending on the Holy Spirit's counsel and living according to the Word of God.

TEMPTED WITH THE SIN OF RACISM

Although my spirit has been perfected, I still have to battle with old thought patterns that are ingrained in my memory. That is why my mind needs to be transformed. As a new creation in Christ, I have been delivered from my past history with racism, but the devil can still tempt me with future encounters with it.

The racial injustice against African Americans has sparked America's racial reckoning that has been past overdue for decades. Because of my past encounters with racism and the emotional pain associated with it, it is easy for me to be tempted to respond out of my emotions when I see it or have an encounter with it, but because of who I am in Christ, I am learning to respond the way God would have me to respond. The only way to do that is through the lens of the Spirit, not through the lens of my experiences. If I don't, Satan can use the sin of racism as a tool to try to enslave me to anger, bitterness, or fear, which make me feel less than who I am in Christ. Thanks to Jesus though, I know who I am, based on my identity in Christ. I don't have to give in to the temptation to think less of myself or feel inadequate even though someone thinks less of me because of the color of my skin.

> THE ONLY WAY TO DO THAT IS THROUGH THE LENS OF THE SPIRIT, NOT THROUGH THE LENS OF MY EXPERIENCES.

THE PSYCHOLOGICAL AND SPIRITUAL BATTLE OF RENEWING OUR MINDS

There is no inequity with God when it comes to humanity. He created us, decided the tone of our skin, and loves everyone with the same love. God's love for us is so rich that He "rescued us from the domain of darkness and transferred us to the kingdom of His beloved Son" (Colossians 1:13). We are no longer "in Adam," or "in the flesh," we are spiritually alive "in Christ" (Romans 8:9). "Therefore, if anyone is in Christ, the new creation has come: the old has gone, the new is here"

> THERE IS NO INEQUITY WITH GOD WHEN IT COMES TO HUMANITY. HE CREATED US, DECIDED THE TONE OF OUR SKIN, AND LOVES EVERYONE WITH THE SAME LOVE.

(2 Corinthians 5:17). "The Spirit himself testifies with our spirit that we are God's child" (Romans 8:16). The moment I became a new creation in Christ, my spirit was made new.

In his book *Secrets to Spiritual Power*, Watchman Nee says, "Outside of Christ, I am only a sinner, but in Christ, I am saved. Outside of Christ, I am empty; in Christ, I am full. Outside of Christ, I am weak; in Christ, I am strong. Outside of Christ, I cannot; in Christ, I am more than able. Outside of Christ, I have been defeated; in Christ, I am already victorious."[1] How meaningful are the words "in Christ?"

However, when we came into this world, we were not in Christ. We were born dead in our trespasses and sin. We had neither the presence of God in our lives nor the knowledge of His ways. Consequently, we learned to live our lives independently of God. One day, we came to Christ, but nobody erased our memory bank. Our minds were still filled with the same old information, whether that information is good or bad. Everything we learned before is still recorded in our minds. The lies we believe about God, family, and ourselves still profoundly influence how we behave and how we live until we change the information. That is why Paul wrote, "Do not conform to patterns of this world but be transformed by the renewing of your mind" (Romans 12:2). As believers, we have to take the responsibility to transform our minds. If we don't, we will live our lives as if we were not made new in Christ.

> AS BELIEVERS, WE HAVE TO TAKE THE RESPONSIBILITY TO TRANSFORM OUR MINDS. IF WE DON'T, WE WILL LIVE OUR LIVES AS IF WE WERE NOT MADE NEW IN CHRIST.

Paul describes this psychological renewing of our minds as a battle. "For though we live in the world, we do not wage war as the world does. The weapons we fight with are not the weapons of the world.

On the contrary, they have divine power to demolish strongholds. We demolish arguments and every pretension that sets itself up against the knowledge of God, and we take captive every thought to make it obedient to Christ" (2 Corinthians 10:3-5). The word stronghold or fortress also had the meaning of prison. What are those strongholds, and how are they raised up against the knowledge of God?

Everything we learned before we came to Christ was assimilated from the environment in which we were raised in two primary ways. First, we developed our worldview from prevailing experiences. By that, we mean the home we were raised in, the friends and relatives we had, the schools we attended, and the church we went to or didn't. It is important to note that two children raised in the same home can, and usually will, respond differently to the same environment due to their personal choices and the uniqueness of their God-given gifts, talents, and potentialities. Imagine that one boy could be raised in a supportive Christian home and believe this world is a pretty good place to live. Another boy doesn't know who his birth father is. His mother has multiple sex partners, and someone physically abused him. What is his perception of this world and himself? Which of those two boys needs Christ more? Both are precisely the same in their need for Christ, and we must never forget that, but they will struggle with different issues.

Second, our worldview is shaped by traumatic experiences such as physical, emotional, or verbal abuse, the death of a loved one, or parents' divorce. It took us years to realize that people are not in bondage to past traumas. They are in bondage to lies they believe because of the trauma, such as, "I'm no good;" "God doesn't love me;" "I'll never measure up;" and "I can't trust anybody." Essentially, we become prisoners to the lies we believe. These "strongholds" are mental patterns of thought burned into our minds over time that produce habits that are deeply embedded in our memories due to past traumas. If you suffered harm for telling the truth, you probably learned to lie or blame others. If you were put down for being emotionally honest, you likely became emotionally isolated and found it difficult to express yourself. Psychologists call such responses "defense mechanisms," and we all have them. Theologians would probably call them "flesh patterns." Both flesh patterns and strongholds represent all learning accomplished independently from God.

Some flesh patterns may appear to be good. Secular counselors operating in the flesh try to help their clients root out defense mechanisms. A major flesh pattern that seems good is self-sufficiency or independence, but it may be our greatest enemy to our dependence on Christ. In hindsight, Stephanie and I, in many ways, tried to fix our marriage in the flesh. We tried hard to stick it out and logically work through our problems. Behind closed doors, nothing we did seemed to work. We prayed, quoted scriptures, talked late hours in the night, and listened to well-respected preachers and teachers. Still, because we didn't know how crucially important it was to resolve our own personal and spiritual conflicts and have a clear understanding of who we were in Christ, we continued to suffer in silence. We both had old habits that were hard to break.

Once we become conditioned to a specific thinking pattern, it can be challenging to reprogram our minds. This is undoubtedly true of thought patterns and habits that we bring into our relationships that are contrary to God's Word. Those old thought patterns and habits don't automatically go away. They are still with us. In order to build healthier relationships, we must learn how to break away from those old thought patterns and habits. How does that happen? Paul called the process renewing our minds. He challenges us to present ourselves and our bodies to God instead of to sin and Satan (Romans 6:12, 13;12:1). Why is renewing the mind so critical? Because no one can consistently live in a way that is inconsistent with how he thinks or perceives himself. You must change your thinking if you are going to change your behavior. Why does our mind work this way? To understand this question, we need to understand how our outer self, our physical body, relates to our inner self, our soul and spirit.

A CHRIST-CENTERED PSYCHOLOGY

Believers are part material and part immaterial, described by Paul as an inner person and an outer person (2 Corinthians 4:16). The two work in unison, and the obvious connection is between the brain and the mind. The brain is part of our physical body (outer person), and our soul is a part of our spiritual body (inner person). Our physical body will return to dust when we physically die. However, as a believer in Christ, our spiritual body will be present with God. However, we won't be mindless because the mind is part of the soul/spirit, as seen below.[2]

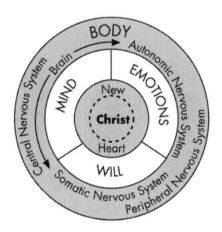

The brain/mind connection is similar to a computer operation with two distinct components: the hardware (brain) and the software (mind). The hardware (brain) is the medical profession's primary focus when treating mental and emotional problems in the mind (software). Taking a pill to cure physical pain for the body is commendable, but taking a pill to heal the soul (mind, emotion, and will) is deplorable. Taking medication for emotional pain is helpful, but it only brings temporary relief that doesn't resolve the core issue, which are spiritual and emotional issues. If we only consulted our Bible, we would conclude that the software (mind) is the primary issue.

Of course, we can have a hardware problem like organic brain disorder, dementia, and chemical imbalances. The software (mind) will not work effectively if the computer (brain) is malfunctioning. It is pretty hard to think clearly, much less pray, while suffering a migraine headache. The brain and the spinal cord make up the central nervous system. Stemming from the peripheral nervous system with two distinct channels, the somatic nervous system regulates all our muscular and skeletal movements. It is that part of our body that we have volitional control over. It obviously correlates with our will.

The autonomic nervous system regulates all our glands, which we don't have direct control over. That correlates with our emotions, which we also don't have direct control over. If you think you do, try telling yourself that you enjoy flying in an airplane if you feel it is dangerous. You can't just decide to change your feelings towards something you believe is hazardous to your well-being. We only have control over what we think and what we choose to believe.

SPIRITUAL THERAPY BRINGS EMOTIONAL STABILITY

To help you understand how it all fits together, let me give you a story about my first trip to Africa and how I dealt with stress. God created us with the ability to withstand a certain amount of stress. I like traveling with my wife, but my wife loves to travel. She has been flying in airplanes since she was a little girl. On the other hand, my first experience on a plane wasn't until I was nineteen years old. One year we went on a work trip to Africa. My initial feelings about the trip were excitement because I had always wanted to go to Africa, but the more time I had to think about flying and the possibility of what could happen while flying, I became more anxious. When the time finally came for our trip, I was a little uptight, but my wife was relaxed because of her flying experience. When we took off for Africa, my adrenal glands responded by discharging cortisol-like hormones into my bloodstream. That adrenalin rush equips us with a flight or fight response. Physically, every time the plane would fly through a cloud or hit an air pocket, I wanted to get off the plane. On the other hand, my wife was fast asleep and barely moved. If I didn't control my thoughts, stress could turn into distress, and I could become physically sick. So, to change my thoughts and calm my body, I began to listen to some music. I chose to listen to some of my favorite artists: Fred Hammond, Cece Winans, Commissioned, and Kirk Franklin, to calm my body.

Why was it that my wife and I had such different responses to the same flight experience? Stephanie slept through turbulence, and I was stressed. Is it because she has superior adrenal glands? No, because if she saw a bug in our home, her response to that bug would be different than mine. There might be some physical differences, but the primary difference is how we mentally process information.

Consider the Philistines and the Israelites who were about to head into battle. When the Philistines offered a "winner takes all" challenge between their champion and anyone the Israelites put forward, the adrenal glands of the Israelites started pumping away. Nobody wanted to step forward and face Goliath. Then along came David who said, "Who is this uncircumcised Philistine, that he should taunt the armies of the living God?" (1 Samuel 17:26) and killed Goliath. Both David and the Israelites had the same data to work with, but they interpreted it differently. David saw Goliath in relation to God, and the others saw Goliath in relation to themselves. Such acts of faith don't happen in a vacuum. The context reveals that David had already seen God deliver him from a lion and a bear.

Let's put it together. The Israelites saw the giant and heard his boasting through their natural senses, and that information was sent to the brain. But it was the mind that interpreted the data which determined the signal sent to the adrenal glands. The brain doesn't tell the mind what to do. The mind tells the brain what to do, and the brain cannot function any other way than how it is programmed. People are not affected by their environment; they are affected by how they perceive or what they believe about what is happening around them. Saying to someone, "You shouldn't feel that way," should be taken from our vocabulary because people can't volitionally change how they feel. It is a subtle form of rejection. It is more appropriate to say, "I'm not sure you understand all the facts because you would probably feel differently if you did understand."

> **THE BRAIN DOESN'T TELL THE MIND WHAT TO DO. THE MIND TELLS THE BRAIN WHAT TO DO, AND THE BRAIN CANNOT FUNCTION ANY OTHER WAY THAN HOW IT IS PROGRAMMED.**

The common tendency is to think that certain activating events are what caused us to feel a certain way, such as, "You did that, and it made me mad," or "You are really getting on my last nerve." Between any activating event and the emotional response is our mental evaluation. Generally speaking, our emotions are a product of our thought life. If what we believe does not conform to truth, then what we feel does not conform to reality. The mind does not deal well with unknowns and characteristically makes assumptions to fill where facts are missing. Human nature usually assumes the worst.

Before flying on an airplane, I came up with my own conclusions about flying because I did not know what to expect. My wife did not have to come up with her own conclusions or expectations because of her previous flying experiences. Over the years, I have learned to appreciate flying because it is not as bad as I imagined. With time and experience, my thoughts and feelings about flying have slowly conformed to reality because I now believe what is true.

COGNITIVE BEHAVIOR THERAPY

Cognitive Behavior Therapy (CBT) is the most entrenched methodology of secular and Christian counselors. The basic theory for (CBT) is that people feel what they are feeling and do what they are doing because of what they have chosen to think and believe.[3] Therefore, if you want to change people's behavior and emotional states, you should seek to change what they believe and consciously choose to think. From a truly Christian perspective, CBT is repentance, which literally means a change of mind. We generally agree with the basic premise of CBT. However, we will explain why secular and secularized

Christian practices of CBT are inadequate in the coming chapters. One glaring omission is that it usually overlooks the spiritual world's reality, which we will briefly address later in this chapter.

In a general sense, believers possess two plans in their minds. Plan B is how they learned to live their lives independently of God, i.e., their flesh patterns. Believers also have a Plan A, which is God's way, because they have the mind of Christ (1 Corinthians 2:16) and the presence of the Holy Spirit who will lead them into all truth. Every believer has a choice. We can choose to walk after the flesh or walk after the Spirit (Galatians 5:16-23). Our choices become evident by the deeds of the flesh or by the fruit of the Spirit. The goal is to be transformed by the renewing of the mind and learn to walk by the spirit and not carry out the desires of the flesh (vs. 16).

Consider God's Plan A for marriage, which is a lifelong monogamous relationship between one man and one woman until death breaks the covenant of either spouse. Premarital counseling should make that clear, but the couple should also be encouraged not to entertain thoughts contrary to that commitment because that is where the battle is won or lost. The temptation may begin with the thought, "I wonder what it would be like to be married to him or her?" Everything after that thought is pure fantasy. One can actually carry on an affair in their mind and emotionally bond to the person of their "fantasies."

If we choose Plan B, which we will be tempted to do, and act upon it for six weeks, we will establish a habit. The result is a mental stronghold. It is like driving a truck along the same route through a pasture for several weeks. Deep ruts are made when the rain comes. Before long, the driver doesn't even need to steer because the truck will naturally follow those ruts. Any attempt to navigate out of them will be met with resistance. In the same way, flesh patterns are information pathways in the brain that have been formed from following the same route.

If we have been trained wrong, can we be retrained? If we programmed our "computer" wrong, can we reprogram it? If we believed a lie, can we renounce that lie and choose to accept the truth? Absolutely, but we must want and choose to change. We are being transformed by renewing our minds every time we listen to a good message, read our Bibles, and seek counsel from godly people.

That is not all that is going on. We are not just up against the world and the flesh. We are up against the world, the flesh, *and* the devil. If we want to mature in Christ, we must reprogram our minds (computers), but we had better check for "viruses." Computer viruses are not accidental. Disgruntled employees and criminal hackers have maliciously implanted them.

Mental strongholds, also known as flesh patterns or defense mechanisms, are developed over time by what we allow ourselves to think every moment of every day. In the second half of 2 Corinthians 10:5, the verb "take" is in the present tense. "We take captive every thought [*noema*] to make it obedient to Christ." The word noema only occurs about six times in Scripture, of which five are in this epistle.[4] It can be translated as "thought," "mind," and "schemes." The way it is used reveals the spiritual battle for our minds. Paul wrote, concerning the need to forgive, "I have forgiven in the sight of Christ for your sake, in order that Satan might not outwit us. For we are not unaware of his schemes [*noema*]" (2 Corinthians 2:10-11). We will not be able to set captives free or heal the wounded without helping them forgive others as Christ has forgiven them. Satan will take advantage of our bitterness. We are cautioned not to let a root of bitterness spring up, causing trouble and defiling many (see Hebrews 12:15). Remember, wounds that are not healed are transferred to others.

Concerning salvation, Paul wrote, "[Satan] has blinded the minds [*noema*] of unbelievers, so that they cannot see the light of the gospel that displays the glory of Christ, who is the image of God" (2 Corinthians 4:4; see also 3:14, in which "minds" is also *noema*). We would understand the need for prayer and pray differently if we understood how Satan blinds unbelievers' minds and thoughts. Evangelism was most effective in the early church which understood how to free people from demonic influences. Being able to do so became a test of righteousness and orthodoxy (see Luke 9:37-43).

For the fifth usage of *noema* in this epistle, Paul wrote, "But I am afraid that just as Eve was deceived by the serpent's cunning, your minds [*noema*] may somehow be led astray from your sincere and pure devotion to Christ" (2 Corinthians 11:3). Satan deceived Eve, and she believed his lies. The tendency is to think that if we are nice people, such deception can't happen to us; but Eve was sinless when she was deceived. Good people can be deceived. Note the spiritual context when Paul used the word *noema* in 2 Corinthians. Clearly, good people can be deceived.

The final use of the word *noema* is found in Philippians 4:6-7: "Do not be anxious about anything [i.e., don't be double-minded], but in every situation, by prayer and petition, with thanksgiving, present your requests to God. And the peace of God, which transcends all understanding, will guard your hearts and your minds [*noema*] in Christ Jesus." In order to stand against Satan's mental assaults, we must choose to think about "whatever is true, whatever is noble, whatever is right, whatever is pure, whatever is lovely, whatever is admirable—if anything is excellent or praiseworthy—think about such things" (vs. 8). In other words, we must learn to "think about what we are thinking about." Then we must put our righteous thoughts into practice, "and the God of peace will be with [us]" (vs. 9).

In one sense, it doesn't make any difference whether the thoughts are coming from our flesh patterns, from the world, or from the father of lies. We examine every thought, and if it is not valid, we don't think about it—and we don't believe it. However, we must learn to separate our thoughts from the enemy's thoughts, or we are going to be deceived and defeated. We have met with hundreds of believers who hear voices or struggle with condemning and blasphemous thoughts. It has proven to be a spiritual battle for their minds in almost every case. Such people are not going to grow in their faith until that is dealt with through genuine repentance and faith in God, including submitting to God and resisting the devil, in that order (James 4:7).

We are not the only people or ministry dealing with this battle for people's minds. All psychiatrists and professional counselors have clients who are experiencing mental struggles. Most would understand such symptoms as the product of a chemical imbalance, but honest questions need to be asked. How can a chemical produce a personality or a thought? How can our neurotransmitters randomly create a thought that we are opposed to thinking? There is no natural explanation. Secularists will likely say that the voices stopped or diminished when the client is given anti-anxiety medication. That is possible, but the whole mental process stopped. All the process did was numb or dull the mental and emotional senses. Take away the medication, and the thoughts are back. Nothing was cured; it was only covered up. The cause was never determined, and only the symptoms were dealt with. Having no mental peace is a primary reason people drink or take drugs. They can drown out those thoughts for a short period of time, but reality sets in the following day.

Can the evil one actually implant a thought in our minds? We wouldn't have had a clue how to answer that question before attending a Freedom In Christ conference. Consider the Old Testament passage, 1 Chronicles 21:1: "Satan rose up against Israel and incited David to take a census of Israel." This was no verbal exchange. These were David's thoughts, or at least he thought they were his. Satan is not going to try to persuade someone like David, who had a heart for God, to follow the pagan practices of his day and sacrifice his babies. He will try to entice God's people to rely on their resources instead of God's resources, which David did, even though the captain of his guard saw it as sin and tried to persuade him otherwise. Thousands died as a result of David being deceived.

Consider the deception of one of Jesus' own disciples: "The evening meal was in progress, and the devil had already prompted Judas, the son of Simon Iscariot, to betray Jesus" (John 13:2). Judas was a thief, and that may be why he was vulnerable, but that flesh pattern does not explain the origin of his plan to betray Jesus. That idea came from Satan. Consider the early church's account of Ananias and Sapphira, who kept for themselves half their profits but wanted the others to think they had given all they had. "Then Peter said, 'Ananias, how is it that Satan has so filled your heart that you have lied to the Holy Spirit and have kept for yourself some of the money you received for the land'" (Acts 5:3)? The word "filled" in this passage is the same as Ephesians 5:18, where we are admonished to "be filled with the Spirit." Whatever we yield ourselves to is what will fill and control us. If every believer were struck dead for that sin as Ananias and Sapphira were, our churches would be empty. Why the severity of discipline? God had to send an early warning to the Church because He knows what the real battle is. If the father of lies can enter your life, marriage, home, or church undetected and persuade you to believe a lie, he can gain some control over your life.

How do we make sense of people hearing voices that others don't hear and seeing things that others don't see? In order to physically hear something, there has to be a source for the sound traveling through the medium of air. People cannot speak in space because sound requires the physical components of air, and in space there is no air. The sound hits our eardrums and sends a signal to our brains. In order to physically see something, there has to be a light source reflecting off a material object back to our optic nerve, which sends a signal to our brain. What these people are struggling with cannot be explained in the natural realm; we have to take into account the unseen spiritual realm, "for our struggle is not against flesh and blood"(Eph. 6:12).

On two separate occasions, Jesus supernaturally revealed what the Pharisees were doing (John 7:20; John 8:45). We know that God is omnipresent and omniscient, and He knows the thoughts and intentions of our hearts.

But the Pharisees didn't know that. For Jesus to have that kind of knowledge, they assumed that He had a demon. Such esoteric knowledge has to have a spiritual origin. In a similar sense, New Agers believe Jesus was the ultimate psychic. Just change the name from "demon" to "spirit guide" and "medium" to "psychic," and a gullible public takes the bait.

We have no idea what is going on in other people's minds unless they have the courage to reveal it, or we have the wisdom to ask the right questions. In our Western culture, most are unlikely to do so because they fear being deemed mentally ill and in need of medication. Medical professionals know that most of their patients are sick for psychosomatic reasons. Their expertise is

> **THE BIBLE IS THE AUTHORITATIVE MANUAL FOR CLEANSING OF THE SPIRIT AND SOUL.**

to restore health to the outer person, but the church has the necessary tools to restore the inner person to a righteous relationship with their Heavenly Father. Mental health care is incomplete without including and understanding the influence of the spiritual realm. The Bible is the authoritative manual for cleansing of the spirit and soul. All that we do is a product of what we think and believe, and the Bible teaches us to meditate on the Word to have success (Joshua 1:8).

CHAPTER 4

Discipleship
Counseling

The church has always been in the business of helping hurting people find their hope and freedom in Christ. When I was a child, the cultural changes and social problems in the U.S. were at an apex and rose to a level that the church wasn't very well equipped to deal with. The civil rights movement peaked in the 1960s with all of its racial tension. The Vietnam War, which my father was drafted into, physically, mentally, and emotionally tore apart thousands of American families. The free sex and drugs movement was born as a revolt against the Vietnam war and dramatically impacted society and the family structure. To meet the many mental and emotional needs from these cultural shifts, the church had to change how it approached ministry. No seminaries or Christian colleges offered doctoral degrees in psychology in those days. However, Bible colleges and seminaries started offering degrees in psychology and marriage and family counseling, but all the professors had secular degrees. In the following years, the church experienced massive growth in programs to deal with mental and emotional issues, but the church also had a corresponding decline in Biblical discipleship. It wasn't intentional, but the focus shifted away from repentance and faith in God to seeking professional counseling to meet people's needs. It is essential to point out that this massive growth in professional counseling is somewhat unique to the United States and Canada, although it has been exported to other countries.

The Bible speaks a lot about the area of psychology and counsel. It speaks with authority about thinking and feeling and pathological problems such as anxiety, depression, anger, unforgiveness, and bitterness. We are told to renew our minds (see Romans 12:2). Transforming our mind is an essential part of the repentance process and a crucial part of becoming mentally and emotionally healthy. In one of our discipleship times, Neil told me about the time he spoke to a large group of pastors in Palm Springs, California. He helped me understand what Biblical counseling, discipleship, and genuine repentance looked like to help others find their freedom in Christ from mental and emotional bondage. He stated that one of his colleagues, Dr. Paul Cedar, closed the session by sharing the story of an African bishop who was visiting the States. In their conversation, the bishop asked, "Why do you have so much counseling in your country?" Paul explained that people in our churches have a lot of problems. The bishop said, "Oh, I see. In America, you counsel people. In Africa, we repent!" Repentance is the crucial part of Biblical discipleship and counseling. An inquirer[8] told her professional Christian counselor that she was going through a repentance process with one of our encouragers. The counselor said, "I don't see how repentance can help you." The further we stray away from Biblical solutions and God's answer to mental and emotional health, the harder we make it on ourselves.

Several years ago, Wheaton College conducted a conference on integrating theology and psychology. Half of the presenters were theologians, and half were psychologists. The conference was titled "The Cure of the Soul." Afterwards, the presentations were published in a book, but with a different title: *Care for the Soul* [1]. The editors of the book explained the change of title. "A number of psychologists at the conference expressed discomfort with the grandiosity implied in 'The Cure of the Soul.' Curing the soul is not the job of psychologists. Surely, Psychologists treat the soul, easing suffering, helping people in emotional pain to reclaim meaning and purpose, and encouraging people to see themselves, others, and the world more accurately. In short, psychologists care for the soul. The cure of the soul, most Christian psychologists would suggest, is God's work and is beyond the scope of mainstream psychological interventions." [2] It is good to recognize our limitations, but if God wants to cure the soul, why are we lowering the standard, especially since God has chosen to work through the Church to accomplish that?

Psychology, by definition, is "the study of the mind and behavior." [3] We are certainly not against that. However, we are not in agreement with secular psychology in the same way that we are not in agreement with liberal theology. In fact, what is needed is a thorough Biblical psychology or anthropology, and we know a lot of professional Christian counselors who feel the same way, but where does one go to get such teaching?

A professional counselor called us and asked for help. He had been hearing voices and had not gotten a good night's rest in nearly two weeks. He was suffering from fear, anxiety, and unresolved personal conflicts from his childhood and was on the verge of a nervous breakdown. For years, to feel loved and valued, he would give of himself and his resources until he was mentally and emotionally drained. He could not keep up with that pace in his life and would burn himself out. He was trying to find his identity by serving and giving to others, but he gave people the power to determine his value. Seeking others' approval gives them the power to tell you who you are, but knowing who you are gives you the power to stop seeking others' approval.

After talking to him and taking him through *The Steps to Freedom,* we explained to him that there is a spiritual side to mental health that involves the demonic and requires genuine repentance and faith in God in order to experience true freedom. As we began walking with him, several things started to happen. He began to believe the truth of God's Word. He began to understand who he was in Christ! He began to believe as a child of God that he had authority over the lies of the enemy and that he was being deceived by the lies he was listening to in his mind. As a professional counselor, why didn't he see it before? Most professional counselors are trained to analyze, understand, explain, and help people cope with their problems. The devil does not care. Satan's first objective is to remain hidden to continue his covert activities. The conflict's true nature becomes apparent when lies are exposed and inquirers are working toward a resolution.

> **SEEKING OTHERS' APPROVAL GIVES THEM THE POWER TO TELL YOU WHO YOU ARE, BUT KNOWING WHO YOU ARE GIVES YOU THE POWER TO STOP SEEKING OTHERS' APPROVAL.**

The same is true for professional pastors. Suppose all we are doing is preaching and teaching to help people make it from one Sunday to the next. In that case, it is unlikely that we will see any demonic manifestations or be aware of any spiritual opposition. Meanwhile, the client in the chair and church members sitting in the pew are mentally struggling with ungodly thoughts. My wife and I have led hundreds through *The Steps to Freedom in Christ* and are training individuals and laypeople in churches to disciple others. Knowing what we know now and what we knew before understanding our identity in Christ, we recognize many pastors and leaders have very little understanding of what is going on in their congregants' minds.

We didn't realize the battle for people's minds when we first started ministry. We didn't even understand it in our own lives. After a morning service, a middle-aged man privately said, "Pastor, I have this voice in my head." At the time, we had no idea what that was, and even if we did, we wouldn't have known what to do about it. So, we helplessly watched his marriage and family fall apart and him leave the Church.

After attending a Freedom in Christ conference, a young man said he had recently enrolled in a secular five-year Doctor of Psychology program and wondered if we would advise against that. Should a believer spend $200,000 and five years of their life learning how to teach people to live independently of God? Most secular schools teach methods that do not include Biblical counsel or use scripture as a foundation. Secular psychology makes sense if there are only natural people living in a natural world excluded from the reality of the spiritual world, which is impossible. Secular psychology is incomplete without teaching or recognizing a Biblical worldview and God's Word.

GOD'S SOVEREIGNTY AND HUMAN RESPONSIBILITY

What sets Biblical counseling and discipleship apart from secular counseling and mentoring is a Christian worldview and the inclusion of

God in the process. Since God is omnipresent, we have to understand our role in relationship with Him. We believe there is a precise line between God's sovereignty and human responsibility. The line will be a little blurred for us, and the Calvinist and the Armenian will adjust the line to the left or the right. However, both theological perspectives acknowledge that Scripture teaches God's sovereignty and human responsibility. On the left side of the line is what God, and only God, can do. We can be creative, but we can't speak and bring something into existence out of nothing. We can't even save ourselves. God created the universe, and He accomplishes His purposes by working through His created order. The providence of God refers to His direction and care over all creation. God "sustains all things by his powerful Word" (Hebrews 1:3). He is the ultimate reality, and if He disappeared, so would all creation. We fulfill our purpose when we live in harmony with Him. We do that by knowing Him and His ways and living according to Biblical truth by faith.

GOD'S SOVEREIGNTY | HUMAN RESPONSIBILITY[4]

Everything on the right side of the line depicts human responsibility. We don't believe that we can pray and ask God to do for us what he told us to do. If you have an important exam tomorrow, you can't ask God to study for you. He told you to "study in order to present yourself approved to God as a workman who does not need to be ashamed" (2 Timothy 2:15 KJV). You can't ask God to think for you. He told us "to think of yourself with sober judgment" (Romans 12:3). We have to assume our responsibility for our thoughts, attitudes, and actions.

Suppose you have a problematic person in your church and some well-meaning Christians ask God to remove him from your fellowship, and nothing happens. Why not God? Don't you love your church? The church is His body, which Jesus paid the ultimate price for, but God told us to go to such a person in private for the purpose of restoration, and if they don't repent, then bring two more witnesses to confront the person (Matthew 18:15-18). The person should be removed from fellowship if there is no repentance. Will God assume our responsibility if we don't? It's not likely that He will go against His Word.

Suppose someone is frightened by some spiritual manifestation in their room and cries out, "God, do something," and nothing happens. So, the person hides under the covers and wonders, "Why not, God? Why are you not helping me? You are all-powerful. Don't you see what is happening to me? Don't you love me? Maybe I'm not a Christian, and that is why God doesn't answer." That was my story as I (Daryl) begged God for help. That is the mental and emotional state of most people we have worked with. They are questioning God's presence, questioning His love for them, and questioning their salvation, but why didn't God do something? He did. There is a part that He and only He could do! He disarmed the devil, forgave our sins, made us new creations in Christ, and positioned us with Christ in the heavenly realms at the Father's right hand. Whose responsibility is it to submit to God and resist the devil? Whose responsibility is it to put on the armor of God, take every thought captive to the obedience of Christ, stand firm in our faith, and make no provision for the flesh in regard to its lusts? That is a part that I and only I must do! If we don't assume our responsibility, we can't assume that there won't be any negative consequences.

WHO IS RESPONSIBLE FOR WHAT?

When we are asked to help another individual, we do so with the awareness that God is always present and that there is a role only He can play in the other person's life. In the following diagram, there is another relationship that exists. That is between the encourager and the inquirer, the discipler and the disciple. Think of it as a triangle with God at the top.[5]

Each side of the triangle represents a relationship. The most important one is our own relationship with God. We need to make sure that the barriers to an intimate relationship with God have been removed through our own repentance. It is also crucial how we relate to the inquirer. Secular counselors focus all their attention on that relationship because their relationship with God and their client's relationship with God is usually not considered. Most have learned how not to be a rescuer, enabler, or co-dependent. They have also developed skills like accurate empathy, congruence, genuineness, and concreteness. Those are good pastoral skills that we can learn from, but they have left out God.

With the triangle in mind, consider who is responsible for what. Many problems in our homes, marriages, and ministries would disappear if we had a balanced answer to that question. Have you ever tried to play the role of the Holy Spirit in the life of your spouse? Your staff? An inquirer?

How did that work for you? We have done it, and, to be honest, it is emotionally, mentally, and physically draining! There is a role that God and only God can play in another's life, and we will fail miserably if we try to take on His role in the process. Have you ever tried to assume another person's responsibility? We have done it. If they wouldn't think or make decisions for themselves, we have made the mistake of doing their thinking and deciding for them in our zeal to help them be healthy. As a result, they became more dependent upon us instead of God.

What are we actually trying to accomplish? What is the primary ministry of the Church? We believe Paul answers the question in 2 Corinthians 5:17,18, "Therefore if anyone is in Christ, the new creation has come; the old has gone, the new is here. All this is from God, who reconciled us to himself through Christ and gave us the ministry of reconciliation." In other words, the ministry of those who are reconciled to God is to help others to be reconciled to God, i.e., to have an intimate relationship with their heavenly Father through genuine repentance and faith in God.

Discipleship is a ministry of reconciliation. The whole world is in a mess because of the fall, and God has only one Plan A, which is to reestablish fallen humanity and present them complete in Christ (Colossians 1:28). Jesus said, "The time has come, the kingdom of God has come near. Repent and believe the good news" (Mark 1:15). The big question is: Do we really believe that repentance and faith in God are the means by which we resolve personal and spiritual conflicts? The answer is no if we usurp each other's roles and fail to include God in the process. The answer is yes if we acknowledge God's role and assume responsibility for ours.

> THERE IS A ROLE THAT GOD AND ONLY GOD CAN PLAY IN ANOTHER'S LIFE, AND WE WILL FAIL MISERABLY IF WE TRY TO TAKE ON HIS ROLE IN THE PROCESS.

INQUIRER'S RESPONSIBILITY (ROLE OF THE DISCIPLE)

We can't do anything about the sovereignty of God other than to teach it and rest in the finished work of Christ. Be assured that God will always do His part, so the remaining question is the role responsibilities of the inquirer (disciple) and the encourager (discipler). To separate the two roles, consider James 5:13-16. The tendency for people in ministry is to see this passage from their perspective and see only the righteous man's role. What gets overlooked is the responsibility of the one seeking help, and if that responsibility is not assumed, the prayers of righteous people will not accomplish much (vs. 16).

The passage begins with, "Is anyone among you in trouble? Let them pray." Initially, the one who should be praying is the inquirer. Why? Because nobody else can do their praying for them. Please understand us. We believe in intercessory prayer, but that was never meant to replace an individual's responsibility to pray. Christians are children of God, and they all have the same access to their heavenly Father. To illustrate, I have four daughters. When my daughters were younger, they loved hanging out and spending the night out with our friend Rachael, who is like another daughter to us. Sometimes our daughters would let Rachael come and beg on their behalf to let them spend the night. That secondhand relationship sometimes worked to their benefit, but that was not the norm with our relationship. No good father accepts a secondhand relationship with his children. Indeed, he wants a close intimate relationship where they can talk openly and honestly with one another.

Years ago, when Stephanie and I began working together to help people, God began sending all kinds of hurting people to us. We were in church trying our best to help people, but inevitably we would get stuck while trying to help them. When we started implementing the seven *Steps to Freedom*, we would tell inquirers, "We don't know how to help you, but God does." So rather than us trying to do their praying for them, we had them pray, and right in front of us, we saw the Holy Spirit begin to help them. Our effectiveness and our role in helping others in ministry changed forever. We were amazed to see how effective it was. We were also amazed to see how light the burden was when we did not take on the work of the Holy Spirit. When they asked God to reveal to their minds who they needed to forgive, names of people surfaced who hadn't been a part of our conversation until then. Their repentance was genuine, and the results lasted because it was God who was leading the process. It was the inquirers who were doing the repenting; we were just there facilitating. We had the privilege of seeing people's lives transformed right in front of us as they were reconciled to God.

A young African American college graduate was sent to me (Daryl) because he was looking for help. On our first meeting, he shared about the dysfunctionality in his home. He could never seem to win the approval of his father. He tried through sports and academics to accommodate and please his father. He got engaged to be married but broke it off because he just didn't feel adequate and could not seem to make the right decisions to get his life together. When he came to see me in my office, he was depressed, lethargic, and full of anxiety about being in any relationship. He had a poor self-image, but a poor self-image is a symptom and not the cause. Most presenting problems are symptomatic; even professional counselors are fully aware of this. In fact, a primary goal of psychotherapy is to identify root causes. After discipling hundreds of people, I knew that forgiving his father was an essential step in helping him get free from his past and move forward. I knew he needed to pray and asked God to reveal to his mind whom he needed to forgive, and he did so. He mentioned his father first, but more names came to his mind: his mother, grandmother, fiancé, and many other people. The young man cried in disbelief as he felt the weight of "performance" lifted from his shoulders. If I had just told him that he needed to forgive his father, I would have known about the father and would not have had a clue about the others, but God did! What are the chances that he would have walked away without dealing with the rest of those individuals? What if I had taken on the role of the Holy Spirit and just dealt with the forgiveness issue with his father? After walking with me for about a year, he went to his ex-fiancé and explained all that had been going on and apologized. Several months later, Stephanie and I attended their wedding.

> **" THESE ARE GOD'S CHILDREN WE ARE WORKING WITH, AND GOD KNOWS EVERYTHING ABOUT THEM. GOD WILL CONVICT THEM OF SIN, SO WE DON'T HAVE TO DO THAT. "**

These are God's children we are working with, and God knows everything about them. God will convict them of sin, so we don't have to do that. With the exception of church discipline, we don't point out sin in other people because we have found it counterproductive. It misdirects that person's battle with God onto us. When conviction comes from God, the power to change comes with it. When they pray and ask God to reveal to their minds how they have been misguided, deceived, rebellious, or prideful, for example, it is incredible what surfaces. We commonly hear inquirers say, "I have never shared this with anyone ever before." Such revelations have very little to do with our unique gifts and abilities. They have petitioned God, and He is surfacing all the issues that need resolution.

There are three questions that Neil asks leaders all over the world. First, how many of you would be willing to share all the dirt in your lives just for the purpose of sharing it? Nobody raises their hand, except for an occasional exhibitionist. Second, how many would be willing to share all the dirt in your lives for the purpose of gaining some understanding as to why you are all screwed up? A few will raise their hands, but even then, somewhat reluctantly. That is as far as secular counseling can take anyone. The goal is to develop trusting relationships, draw as much information as possible out of the clients, and explain why they feel and act the way they do. They can't go any further than that without the gospel. Without the gospel, we are just products of our past, and we need to learn how to live with that reality.

Third, how many of you would be willing to share all of the dirt in your lives in order to resolve it? Everyone's hand goes up. We are not just products of our past. We are new creations in Christ. We can't fix our past, and God chooses not to. Instead, He sets us free from it. When we repent and seek God, He brings to mind all the issues that keep us from having an intimate relationship with our Heavenly Father. Resolution takes place the moment we begin the repentance process.

James continues, "Is anyone among you sick? Let them call the elders of the Church to pray over them and anoint them with oil in the name of the Lord." (vs.14). God puts the responsibility on the one seeking help to take the initiative. We will never see wholeness, health, and freedom in our churches unless we help people realize that gaining those things is their responsibility. We can't be healthy for other people. We can't repent or believe for them, but godly elders can help them by being equipped to offer them that opportunity.

James adds another qualifier, "Therefore, confess your sins to each other and pray for each other so that you may be healed. The effective prayer of a righteous man can accomplish much" (vs.16). A righteous person's prayer doesn't accomplish much until the person they are praying for is right with God. Suppose a person in your church calls the elders for prayer, and the elders take that responsibility very seriously. They agree to fast for a day before they anoint the person with oil and fervently pray for healing. Later they discover that the person is in bondage to bitterness and has many other unresolved spiritual issues in their life. Should we expect God to answer those prayers for healing when they haven't assumed their responsibility? We don't think so. If we really cared for such people, we would help them resolve those conflicts first. Then watch how effective our prayers become.

A lady came to one of our offices desperately asking for help. She said she had deep spiritual conflicts. After sharing her story, she said, "God promised prosperity and good health in 3 John 2. Why isn't that happening?" We told her to finish the verse. "Just as your soul prospers." She had had two abortions and years of drug abuse. How do you think her soul was doing? A similar faulty perspective can be derived from Psalm 37:4, "Take delight in the Lord, and he will give you the desires of the heart." False prophets say, "Claim that promise folks. God will give you the desires of your heart if you would only believe. So, name it and claim it, but you won't get what you want if you don't believe hard enough." If you delight yourselves in the Lord, your desires will change. If you don't first delight yourselves in the Lord, your desires will be of the flesh, and they cannot be satisfied (Psalm 37:3, 5-9).

ENCOURAGER'S RESPONSIBILITY (ROLE OF THE DISCIPLER)

This is the critical passage describing the role of the encourager: "The Lord's bond-servant must not be quarrelsome, but be kind to all, able to teach, patient when wronged, with gentleness correcting those who are in opposition, if perhaps God may grant them repentance leading to the knowledge of the truth, and they may come to their senses and escape from the snare of the devil, having been held captive by him to do his will" (2 Timothy 2:24-26 NASB).

People's lives are like a house where the garbage isn't taken out for months. This attracts a lot of flies. Understandably, the natural response is to get rid of the flies, but what we really should get rid of is the garbage. We know that some ministries study the flies' flight patterns, try to get their names and rank, and attempt to cast them out. There may be some value in doing that, which we are not aware of, but we believe that repentance and faith in God have been and will continue to be the answer throughout the church age. We can chase off the flies, but they will likely tell seven others where the garbage is. Getting rid of the garbage gets rid of the flies.

The encourager only has to work with the inquirer. They can do so without any demons manifesting themselves because the devil isn't the issue. The real issue is our relationship with God. Our goal is for God to reveal himself, and then he is glorified. Divine revelation is the basis for all that we believe, but what makes our ministry effective is the presence of God. When walking with others, we have to avoid being quarrelsome and be kind, patient, and gentle. We also have to know the truth because the truth sets us free.

The Bible doesn't judge the thoughts and intentions of the heart. God does. Jesus is the Truth and the Word. If we use God's Word for just an intellectual pursuit of knowledge, it is no longer living. Christianity is not a better philosophy to live by; it is a personal relationship with the Living God. Paul warns us that "knowledge makes arrogance, but love edifies" (1 Corinthians 8:1). When we make knowledge an end in itself, we undermine the purpose for which it was intended. "But the goal of our instruction is love from a pure heart and a good conscience and a sincere faith" (1 Timothy 1:5). A person can know the Bible and be arrogant because knowledge puffs up, but we can't know God and be arrogant. "All Scripture is inspired by God and profitable for teaching, for reproof, for correction, for training in righteousness" (2 Timothy 3:16). Too often, we have used scripture for teaching and training in competence. Reproof and correction are essential for training in righteousness. The great commission to make disciples comes with the assurance that "I am with you always, even to the end of the age" (Matthew 28:20).

We make every effort to practice the presence of God when we disciple others. To accomplish this, we must be the Lord's bond-servant, i.e., we must be dependent upon God. Discipleship Counseling is an encounter with God, not an encounter with how much Bible we can quote to people. He is the One who grants repentance, and God is the only One who can set captives free and heal the wounds of the broken-hearted. We are not the Wonderful Counselor; God is. We can't change anyone's life; God can and does. We can't usurp the Holy Spirit's role of convicting us of sin and leading us into all truth, nor should we overlook the possibility that the inquirer could be paying attention to a deceiving spirit (see 1 Timothy 4:1). We are just instruments in His hands, trying our best to reconcile children of God with their Heavenly Father.

100

CHAPTER 5

A Discipleship Strategy

What percentage of the people in your church know who they are in Christ, understand what it means to be a child of God, have a devotional and prayer life, are healthy mentally, emotionally, and spiritually, and are bearing fruit? How many are still struggling in their spiritual growth? Paul comments on such carnality in 1 Corinthians 3:1-3 (NASB), "And I, brethren, could not speak to you as to spiritual men, but as to men of flesh, as to infants in Christ. I gave you milk to drink, not solid food, for you were not able to receive it. Indeed, even now, you are not yet able, for you are still fleshly. For since there is jealousy and strife among you, are you not fleshly, and are you not walking like mere men?" We will continue to have "infants in Christ" sitting in our churches, "not able to receive" good messages unless there is some way to resolve such conflicts. Hence the need for genuine repentance.

When Stephanie and I first heard Freedom in Christ's message, we were Christians but infants in our understanding of who we were in Christ. Although we had been Christians for years, we still had not overcome the spiritual trauma from our childhoods. After attending Neil's conference, we began to understand and experience a level of freedom in Christ that we never understood before. I (Daryl) began to feel confident in God's power and love for me, His child. I didn't feel as if God was judging me, which I had always felt going to church. I no longer felt rejected for not being perfect. I was learning to live under the new covenant of grace and began to understand the magnitude and sacrifice of what Jesus did for me. The Lord had already changed me from the inside out from a sinner to a saint. Now He was spiritually teaching me to live out my sainthood by obeying the truth of His word through being led by the power of the Holy Spirit.

> **" THE LORD HAD ALREADY CHANGED ME FROM THE INSIDE OUT FROM A SINNER TO A SAINT. NOW HE WAS SPIRITUALLY TEACHING ME TO LIVE OUT MY SAINTHOOD. "**

I cried and rejoiced for days as I began to understand God's love for me and my identity as His son! The truth was setting me free (John 8:32). I expressed to Neil that I would love for people in the African American community to understand and experience the reality of who they are in Christ. I wanted to learn everything I needed to learn to help others find their freedom.

When Stephanie and I became a part of the Freedom in Christ team in 2016, we were asked to go to London, England to shoot a Freedom in Christ discipleship course designed to help believers of all backgrounds know what it means to be a child of God. Along with the international staff, we have developed a 10-week discipleship course entitled the *Freedom In Christ Course* (Bethany House Publishers).[1] Some of the areas covered in the course include:

- How we become brand-new people from the inside out when we become Christians

- Why we can go boldly into God's presence any time we like without fear

- How nothing we do can make God love us any more or any less

- How to resolve the effect of even the deepest issues from the past

- How to deal with repeating patterns of sin

- Understanding what God's purpose is for your life (it may not be what you think!)

This curriculum is ideal for Bible study or other small groups at church or home. To date over 350,000 people have gone through the curriculum in English, and it has been translated into over 25 languages. These numbers continue to grow! Every Christian, including you, is both a disciple and a discipler in the context of his or her Christian relationships. We have the incredible privilege and responsibility to be a teacher and a learner of what it means to be in Christ, walk by faith, and live in the Spirit.

Messages given on Sunday morning are going right over many attendees' heads. As a discipler, you may not have an official responsibility to disciple anyone, but you have the opportunity to help other believers grow in Christ through caring, committed relationships. Many in the Church feel like I did when I was growing up. They stop reading their Bibles because all they see is condemnation. In *The Steps To Freedom In Christ,* there is a page entitled "Statements of Truth," a collection of Scriptural verses stating the truth about God. When I was going through *The Steps* and read through those statements, I made no emotional connection with the content. It felt like I was just reading words. When I finished *The Steps,* the leaders had me return to that page and reread the statements. When I reread them, they connected differently; they read more intimately. The statements did not change, but something changed within me; I changed! Gospel recording artist Tramaine Hawkins wrote a great song called "Changed." Her song describes the freedom found in Christ this way:

> A change, a change has come over me.
> He changed my life, and now I'm free.
> He washed away all my sins, and he made me whole,
> He washed me white as snow.
> He changed, my life complete, and now I sit,
> I sit at His feet. To do what must be done
> I'll work and work until He comes
> A wonderful change has come over me
> Lord, you've changed my life complete.
> I'm so glad you changed me![2]

Now I read the Bible with no condemnation and a complete understanding of who I am in Christ and God's unconditional love for me as His child.

After walking with people and taking them through *The Steps to Freedom,* we sometimes ask, "Now, when you read your Bible, what do you see?" Almost everyone will say, "I'm in Christ! Why couldn't I see that before?" Before repentance, there was very little growth. After repentance and understanding their identity in Christ, they read their Bibles with a different lens and view God differently. Their spiritual growth begins to accelerate.

Before I (Daryl) went through *The Steps,* I thought God only used perfect people. Moses, Joseph, David, Esther, and Mary all seemed to be perfect, which in my mind qualified them to be saints. I thought a saint was a person who, with time and age, learned how to become perfect. As a kid, I remember a section in the church where all the deacons sat. They all were old. I always thought they sat there because they had reached a level of perfection that took years to accomplish. I thought I would never reach that status. In church time and time again, we heard we should all be holy because God is holy (see 1 Peter 1:13). I tried my best, but I failed over and over again. I knew my struggles, and I could not live up to that standard. I dare not say anything while I was at church because it seemed that I was the only one who struggled. Everyone else seemed to have it all together. I gave my heart to Jesus nearly every Sunday because I wanted to be a saint like those old men sitting in the corner. I was also afraid of going to hell. I tried to live right, but it seemed that I was reminded each Sunday that I just wasn't good enough. Because I could not live the holy life, I was afraid to attend church and afraid not to.

> **ALTHOUGH I HAD BEEN A CHRISTIAN FOR MANY YEARS, I WAS NOT FIRMLY ROOTED OR BUILT UP IN HIM. I DID NOT UNDERSTAND WHO I WAS IN CHRIST AND WHAT IT MEANT TO BE A CHILD OF GOD.**

Although I had been a Christian for many years, I was not firmly rooted or built up in Him. I did not understand who I was in Christ and what it meant to be a child of God. But after going through *The Steps* and understanding my identity as a child of God, this all changed. There is nothing "magical" about *The Steps.* It is just a seven-step repentance process led by the Holy Spirit that helps people connect to God.

105

After going through *The Steps to Freedom*, I (Stephanie) knew I had experienced an incredible change. It was as if the blinders had fallen off of my eyes. Because of past painful experiences, I had a tendency to be very skeptical. I had very little trust in those around me. After *The Steps,* I saw believers for who they are in Christ and not through a lens of judgment or condemnation. My heart broke for believers who chose sin because I understood they were walking in blindness just as I had. I desired to be kind, compassionate, and forgiving instead of protective. I wanted others to know the truth. Although I knew I had to grow deeper in my understanding of who I was in Christ, I was excited about what God had done in my life. This change was permanent.

In the Gospels, both Paul and John present three growth levels—children, fathers, and young men—from different perspectives. John wrote, "I am writing to you, little children, because your sins have been forgiven you, on account of his name. I am writing to you, fathers, because you know him who is from the beginning. I am writing to you, young men, because you have overcome the evil one. I write to you, dear children, because you know the Father. I write to you, fathers, because you know him who is from the beginning. I write to you, young men, because you are strong, and the Word of God lives in you, and you have overcome the evil one" (1 John 2:12-14).

Little children have overcome the penalty of sin and have an elementary knowledge of their Father. Fathers have a much deeper, experiential and reverential relationship with their heavenly Father, whom they have known from the beginning. Young men in the faith have "overcome the evil one," a phrase which John repeats twice. They have overcome the power of sin. They no longer have any uncontrollable appetites or addictive behaviors and have overcome the barriers preventing them from having an intimate relationship with their heavenly Father. How will we help our people reach the stature of "young men" if they don't know how to overcome the evil one?

Paul outlines the maturation process in Colossians 2:6,7. "So then, just as you received Christ Jesus the Lord, continue to live your lives in him, rooted and built up in him and strengthened in the faith as you were taught, and overflowing with thanksgiving." New believers must be firmly rooted in Christ in order for them to grow in Christ and live freely in Christ. The next verse describes how *not* to make fruitful disciples, "See to it that no one takes you captive through philosophy and empty deception, according to the tradition of men, according to the elementary principles of the world, rather than according to Christ" (vs. 8). Then Paul comes back to the core issue of Christianity, "For in Christ all the fullness of Deity lives in bodily form, and in Christ, you have been brought to fullness. He is the head over every power and authority" (verses 9,10).

Every aspect of our growth in Christ depends on our union with God. The following chart illustrates what obstacles need to be overcome and lessons need to be learned at various stages of growth: spiritually, rationally, emotionally, volitionally, and relationally.

LEVELS OF CONFLICT[3]

	LEVEL ONE: Rooted in Christ (COLOSSIANS 2:10)	LEVEL TWO: Built-up in Christ (COLOSSIANS 2:7)	LEVEL THREE: Living in Christ (COLOSSIANS 2:6)
SPIRITUAL	Lack of salvation or assurance (EPHESIANS 2:1-3)	Living according to the flesh (GALATIANS 5:19-21)	Insensitive to the Spirit's leading (HEBREWS 5:11-14)
RATIONAL	Pride and ignorance (1 CORINTHIANS 8:1)	Wrong belief or philosophy (COLOSSIANS 2:8)	Lack of Knowledge (HOSEA 4:6)
EMOTIONAL	Fearful, guilty, and shameful (MATTHEW 10:26-33; ROMANS 3:23; ROMANS 8:1-2)	Angry (EPHESIANS 4:31) Anxious (1 PETER 5:7) Depressed (2 CORINTHIANS 4:1-18)	Discouraged and sorrowful (GALATIANS 6:9)
VOLITIONAL	Rebellious (1 TIMOTHY 1:9)	Lack of self-control (1 CORINTHIANS 3:1-3)	Undisciplined (2 THESSALONIANS 3:7,11)
RELATIONAL	Rejected and unloved (1 PETER 2:4)	Bitter and unforgiving (COLOSSIANS 3:13; HEBREWS 12:15)	Selfish (1 CORINTHIANS 10:24; PHILIPPIANS 2:1-5)

Defeated Christians can sit under the teaching of the best Bible teachers and make no progress if they don't know who they are in Christ and how to deal with pride, guilt, shame, fear, rebellion, bitterness, and interpersonal conflicts. The purpose of Discipleship Counseling is to resolve the personal and spiritual conflicts that keep them from being firmly rooted in Christ. Once they are resolved, the growth process is uninhibited. Leading someone through *The Steps* is not an end; it is the beginning of the growth process. The following chart illustrates the growth and functional capability at each level of maturity:

LEVELS OF GROWTH[4]

	LEVEL ONE: Rooted in Christ (COLOSSIANS 2:10)	LEVEL TWO: Built-up in Christ (COLOSSIANS 2:7)	LEVEL THREE: living in Christ (COLOSSIANS 2:6)
SPIRITUAL	Child of God (ROMANS 8:16; 1 JOHN 5:13)	Lives according to the Spirit (GALATIANS 5:19-23)	Led by the Spirit (ROMANS 8:14)
RATIONAL	Desire to know the truth (JOHN 8:32)	Correctly uses the Bible (2 TIMOTHY 2:15)	Adequate and equipped (2 TIMOTHY 3:16-17)
EMOTIONAL	Free in Christ (GALATIANS 5:1)	Joyful, peaceful, and patient (GALATIANS 5:22)	Contented (PHILIPPIANS 4:11)
VOLITIONAL	Submissive (ROMANS 13:1-5)	Self-controlled (GALATIANS 5:22)	Disciplined (1 TIMOTHY 4:7-8)
RELATIONAL	Accepted and forgiven (ROMANS 5:8; 15:7)	Forgiving (EPHESIANS 4:32)	Loving and unselfish (PHILIPPIANS 2:1-5)

Past, present, and future tenses are used in the Bible when referring to believers' salvation. We have been saved (Ephesians 2:5,8; 2 Timothy 1:8,9); we are presently being saved (1 Corinthians 1:18; 2 Corinthians 2:15); and someday we shall be fully saved (Romans 5:9,10; 13:11). As believers, our salvation experience is not yet fully complete, and it won't

> **IT IS OUR RESPONSIBILITY TO WORK OUT IN OUR EXPERIENCE WHAT GOD HAS WORKED IN US THROUGH SALVATION.**

be until we physically die, receive resurrected bodies, and reside fully in the presence of God. However, God desires us to have the assurance of salvation (see 1 John 5:13). There is a "coming wrath" (1 Thessalonians 1:10) of God, but we have the confidence that when that wrath comes, we will be saved from it. Having believed, "You were sealed in him with the Holy Spirit of promise, which is an earnestness of our inheritance, unto the redemption of God's own possession, unto the praise of His glory" (Ephesians 1:13,14 ASV).

Boasting that we have been saved, sealed, and sanctified implies that God's work in our lives is finished. Such erroneous thinking doesn't provide very much motivation to press on in the pursuit of God as the Apostle Paul exhorted us to do in Philippians 3:13,14: "Brothers and sisters, I do not consider myself yet to have taken hold of it. But one thing I do: forgetting what is behind and straining toward what is ahead, I press on toward the goal to win the prize for which God has called me heavenward in Christ Jesus."

If you have been born again, you are indeed in the kingdom of God, but you will likely be stagnant in your growth if you fail to "work out your salvation with fear and trembling" (Philippians 2:12).

Beyond our initial salvation experience, God's will for our lives is our sanctification (1 Thessalonians 4:3), which is also a past, present, and future tense for believers. In other words, believers have been sanctified (1 Corinthians 1:2; 6:11); they are being sanctified (2 Corinthians 7:1; 1 Thessalonians 4:3); and someday they will be fully sanctified (1 Thessalonians 3:12,13; 5:23,24). The sanctifying process begins at our new birth and ends in glorification. The author of Hebrews wrote, "Make every effort to live in peace with everyone and to be holy; without holiness no one will see the Lord" (12:14).

Past tense sanctification is often referred to as positional sanctification, and present tense sanctification is referred to as progressive or experiential sanctification. Holiness churches tend to focus on positional sanctification, and some see sanctification as a done deal, which can lead to serious errors. One man boasted that he hadn't sinned in 20 years. We asked him if his wife would agree with that assessment! "If we claim to be without sin, we deceive ourselves, and the truth is not in us" (1 John 1:8).

Reformed theology focuses on progressive sanctification, implying that sanctification is synonymous with growth or maturity. Positional sanctification is often dismissed as just positional truth, as though it is practically irrelevant. Consequently, many are trying to become someone they already are. Positional sanctification is the basis for progressive sanctification. Christians are not trying to become children of God; they are children of God who are becoming like Jesus. Positional sanctification (who we already are in Christ) is the basis for progressive sanctification (who we are becoming in Christ).

> **CHRISTIANS ARE NOT TRYING TO BECOME CHILDREN OF GOD; THEY ARE CHILDREN OF GOD WHO ARE BECOMING LIKE JESUS.**

ENTRANCE INTO THE CHURCH

Entrance into the early church began with a repentance process followed by baptism. Individuals would literally face the west and renounce Satan and all his works and all his ways. Then they would face the East and make their profession of faith in God. Catholic and Orthodox churches still follow that procedure, but it has been considerably minimized. Some older Protestant liturgical churches still follow that practice as well. The purpose was to publicly say, in essence, "I used to believe a certain way and live accordingly, but now I renounce those beliefs and that way of life. I now choose to trust God, believe His Word, and live accordingly by faith." If their faith was sincere and their repentance genuine, there would be an observable change in their lives and how they lived.

Entrance into some evangelical churches begins with a salvation experience that would appear more like an addition than transformation. Believers just receive Jesus and add Him onto their lives. Without repentance, they still believe what they have always believed, but now they also believe something new as well. We can't believe the truth and a lie simultaneously and expect to grow. If we choose to believe the truth, then there should be a corresponding choice to no longer believe the lies. "You cannot drink the cup of the Lord and the cup of demons too; you cannot have a part in both the Lord's table and the table of demons" (1 Corinthians 10:21). All children of God are positionally alive and free in Christ, but how many live that way? If they want to experience freedom and grow in the grace and knowledge of the Lord Jesus Christ, they need to repent.

STARTING WITH FREEDOM

Very little training is required for mature and Biblically literate pastors to lead an inquirer through *The Steps to Freedom in Christ*. It is a self-guided process that people can complete on their own. Our ministry has received emails and letters from people worldwide who have processed *The Steps* on their own. Years ago, Dr. Wayne Grudem was one of the most widely read systematic theologians in the world. In the forward for Neil's book, *Liberating Prayer*, which includes *The Steps*, Dr. Grudem wrote:[5]

> After living more than 50 years as a Christian, and after teaching more than 25 years as a professor of Bible and theology, I took about two hours to work carefully through Neil's seven Steps to Freedom in Christ and apply each step to my own life, reading each suggested prayer aloud. God used that process to bring to mind a number of thoughts and attitudes that He wanted to correct and then to impart to me a wonderfully refreshing sense of freedom, peace, joy, and fellowship with Himself.

In most cases, we just show up, and God sets us free. However, there are complex cases that require more training. The purpose of Freedom in Christ Ministries is to equip the Church worldwide and enable them to establish their people, marriages, and ministries alive and free in Christ through genuine repentance and faith in God. We are not a counseling ministry, and we will not do your discipling for you, but we will help you equip godly people in your church who can help others. We have offices and representatives worldwide who offer that kind of training.

One of the opportunities we offer is *TRANSFORM*, a journey for Christian leaders into greater freedom, fruitfulness, and disciple-making. It is an 8-to-10-month program (depending on where you live) of weekly study, reflection, and fellowship designed to help ground your leadership firmly in the Biblical principles of identity, freedom, and transformation, confident that this will lead to greater influence and fruitfulness in your life and ministry. Our office in the United States also has an online training program called CFMU for those who want to start a "Freedom Ministry" in their church or community. There are hundreds of associates spread around the U.S. with a built-in network of support, community, and encouragement. Having trained encouragers in a church can take a huge load off the pastor.[7]

For the congregation, we offer several basic discipleship courses that explain creation, the fall, worldview, how to live by faith, mental strongholds, the battle for our minds, emotions, forgiveness, and relationships. The best possible scenario is to plant a church and offer all new members a discipleship class on who they are in Christ and the spiritual battle for the mind. Imagine a church where everyone knows who they are in Christ and has resolved all known personal and spiritual conflicts. However, it is never too late to offer the class in Sunday school, small groups, and home Bible studies. But it can't be a one-time offering because every church has a constant turnover of people. The class should be continuously offered for new members and converts.

OVERCOMING FLESH PATTERNS

The purpose of the *Freedom in Christ Course* is to establish people alive and free in Christ as they submit to God and resist the devil (James

4:7). Neil Anderson with Rich Miller, our past US President, has written a twenty-one-day devotional entitled *Walking In Freedom*.[6] Each day has truth about God, truth about who we are in Christ, and truth about freedom. Every third day readers are encouraged to go through one of the seven Steps again to reinforce what they have previously declared. With the barriers removed between them and God, the life of Christ will empower them to grow and bear fruit. With a quiet and clear mind, they can be transformed by renewing their minds.

However, some people have significant flesh patterns that require additional help to overcome. Most common among them are anger, sexual strongholds, chemical addiction, depression, anxiety disorders, and broken marriages. The rest of this book will include a chapter on each of those issues. Ideally, a church could offer a support group for such personal needs, but if that is not available, we have written books for each of those issues that can be kept in the church library or made available for loan or purchase. We believe that Jesus provides an answer to every problem plaguing humanity through submitting to Him and resisting the Devil in repentance and faith.

CHAPTER 6

Overcoming Anger

At some point in their lives, every person is going to deal with anger. I (Daryl) grew up believing that anger was not to be outwardly expressed because it was a sign of disrespect towards authority. I suppressed my thoughts and feelings, which only made me feel like my voice did not matter. I did not realize the impact that my lack of open communication would have on my marriage and how it would be something Satan would use against my wife and I in our relationship. Whenever Stephanie and I would disagree, I would shut down emotionally and get angry, but my anger would come out in passive-aggressive ways. My conversations with her were short and sarcastic. I was a man of faith, but I did not know how to express my emotions correctly in the context of my faith. I did not understand the interaction between faith and feelings. My faith was misguided because I believed I could not openly share my emotions.

There is no more important issue to grasp than the nature of faith. Faith is the means by which we live and relate to God. We are saved by grace through faith (Ephesians 2:8-9), sanctified by faith (Acts

26:18), and live by faith (2 Corinthians 5:7). "And without faith, it is impossible to please God, because anyone who comes to him must believe that he exists and that he rewards those who earnestly seek him" (Hebrews 11:6). What we believe is directly related to how we live and how we emotionally respond to the circumstances of life. There are three basic principles of faith that, when understood, can keep us on the right path and prevent us from acting presumptuously.

First, faith is dependent upon its object. In reality, everyone lives by faith; it is the operating principle of life. The only difference between Christian faith and non-Christian faith is the object of our faith. The issue is not whether one believes or doesn't believe. The real issue is in what or in whom one believes. One cannot have faith in faith!

Hope is the parent of faith. The Biblical idea of hope is not wishful thinking. Instead, hope is the present assurance of some future good. People don't proceed by faith if they have no hope. Suppose you want to build better race relationships. You're open to developing a friendship with people of a different race, hoping they in turn will want to do the same. You move forward in faith, hoping that the time and effort you put in will develop into a mutual friendship. However, if misunderstanding and constant frustration continues to happen and the relationship stalls, your hope will be shaken, and you will lose faith in building race relations. If you never have any hope of developing a relationship, it would be foolish to proceed by faith. "Now faith is confidence in what we hope for and assurance about what we do not see" (Hebrews 11:1).

God and His Word are the only legitimate objects of our faith because they never change: "Jesus Christ is the same yesterday and today and forever" (Hebrews 13:8). We learn to trust people who are true to their word and in things that have proven to be consistent. It takes time to establish trust in something or someone because the process of building faith requires consistent and continuous behavior demonstrated over time. That is why human relationships are so fragile. It may take months or years to establish a high degree of trust in another person, but one act of unfaithfulness can destroy it. We can choose to forgive those who have betrayed us, but it often takes a long time to regain the trust that has been lost, if it ever happens at all.

Second, how much faith we have depends on how well we know the object of our faith. That is why Christian faith "comes from hearing the message, and the message is heard through the Word about Christ" (Romans 10:17). If we have little knowledge of God and His Word, we can only have a little faith. Stepping out in faith beyond that which we know to be true is presumption. Believing something to be true does not make it true. Jesus is the Truth; therefore, we believe Him, and He would still be the Truth even if we didn't believe Him. We don't create reality with our minds. God is our ultimate reality. Mentally healthy people are in touch with reality.

Third, our actions demonstrate our reliance on the object of our faith. The Greek word for faith is *pistis*, which is a noun. The Greek word for believe and trust is *pisteuo*, a verb. James wrote, "You have faith, and I have works; show me your faith without works, and I will show you my faith by my works" (James 2:18).

People don't always live according to what they profess, but they do live according to their beliefs. Every action is preceded by a thought. Any change of behavior can only be accomplished by changing what one believes. Coercing someone to behave a certain way without having a corresponding inner conviction only teaches them to outwardly act as if they were changed without transforming what they believe.

Any time Stephanie and I had disagreements in our marriage, I felt this uneasy emotional tension rise within myself. I wanted to express myself, but I did not know how to say what I felt because I did not want to disrespect her. I did not understand why it was difficult for me to express my emotions. Time and time again, she would ask me to communicate with her, but I did not know how to verbally say what I felt. So I would get angry, shut down, and become emotionally distant. It was frustrating for me not to know how to express what I was feeling and frustrating for her to feel emotionally rejected. As a child of God, if I did not learn how to handle conflict through God's Word and apply it by faith, it could have caused more problems in our marriage. I would never have learned how to overcome the lies and destructive patterns in my life. Proverbs 27:5 says, "Better is open rebuke (communication) than hidden love."

> **PEOPLE DON'T ALWAYS LIVE ACCORDING TO WHAT THEY PROFESS, BUT THEY DO LIVE ACCORDING TO THEIR BELIEFS. EVERY ACTION IS PRECEDED BY A THOUGHT. ANY CHANGE OF BEHAVIOR CAN ONLY BE ACCOMPLISHED BY CHANGING WHAT ONE BELIEVES.**

We are justified by faith and faith alone. Living by faith demonstrates reliance upon God's Word and not our experiences. "So, in Christ Jesus, you are all children of God through faith" (Galatians 3:26, see also Romans 3:28). If what you profess to believe doesn't affect your walk and your talk, then your faith is only a preference that will dissipate under pressure. Biblical faith is not mental assent to God. It is practically putting our trust in what He says and applying it to everyday life. It has taken some time to transform my mind and overcome my bad habit of being passive-aggressive, but I am learning that having faith in God's Word is better than trusting in my ways.

GOALS AND DESIRES

How does faith, or what we believe, relate to anger, the subject of this chapter? Flesh patterns are all based on faulty beliefs, usually formulated in our minds before we came to Christ. For instance, as a child, I learned how to survive in life through silence by not making waves or drawing attention to myself. It looked as if I were a compliant child. I wasn't mean-spirited; however, my silence and passive-aggressive behavior developed as a means of protecting myself. Paul's list of flesh patterns in Galatians 5:19-21 includes "fits of rage, selfish ambition, dissensions, and factions" (vs. 20). A significant shift in thinking should take place upon conversion. We were heading in one direction based on what we believed and how we learned to live independently of God. If repentance is genuine, it will precipitate a turning from our old thoughts and starting to live by faith according to what God says is true.

Before we knew Christ, we had preconceived notions about living and meeting our own needs of acceptance, security, significance, and success. These are commonly based on worldly standards of appearance, performance, and social status. Take a moment to reflect on how you would complete these statements:

I would be accepted if . . .
I would be secure if . . .
I would be significant if . . .
I would be successful if . . .

However, completing those sentences reveals what you presently believe—your faith—and you are right now living according to that faith. We believe God wants all His children to be accepted, secure, significant, and live successful lives. Surely you don't believe that our loving Heavenly Father wants us to feel rejected, insecure, insignificant or fail in our attempts to do the "good works, which God prepared in advance for us to do" (Ephesians 2:10)! The critical questions are how we define those issues and how we make them accurate in our experience.

Consciously or subconsciously, we begin every day with some idea of what we would like to do and accomplish. Suppose your plan for the day is to drive to a job interview scheduled for 10:00 a.m. You leave early, but a traffic accident has turned the road into a parking lot. The accident has blocked your goal of getting to the interview on time. How do you feel? You arrive late, and the interview is less than definitive. They say they will get back to you within a week. Now how do you feel since your goal is uncertain? This potential job would be a career change and feels like a critical part of your goal to be successful. Finally, they choose someone more qualified and subtly suggest that you should consider another career track. Now how do you feel? It is natural to feel angry when plans or goals are blocked, to feel anxious when they are uncertain, and to feel depressed when they seem impossible.

No God-given goal for our lives can be impossible, uncertain, or blocked. Even the secular world knows that a leaders' authority is undermined if they issue commands that cannot be obeyed. So if God wants something done, it can be done! "For nothing will be impossible with God" (Luke 1:37 NASB), and "I can do all things through Christ who strengthens me" (Philippians 4:13, NKJV). However, "all things" have to be consistent with God's will.

To understand how we can successfully live the Christian life, we need to distinguish between godly goals and personal desires. *A godly goal is any specific situation that reflects God's purpose for our lives that is not dependent on people or circumstances beyond our right or ability to control.* The only person we have the right and the ability to control is ourselves. Nobody and nothing can keep us from being the person God created us to be, and that is God's goal for our lives. Circumstances should never define who we are, nor should we allow other people to have that kind of power over us. Only God has the right to determine who we are.

When Stephanie and I got married, our goal was to have a loving, harmonious, happy, Christian marriage and family. But because of our own unresolved personal conflicts, we both contributed to blocking that goal. Neither one of us knew how to seek God's goal for our marriage. God's goal for our life, marriage, and family is to become the father and husband or mother and wife God created us to be. We were the only ones who could block that goal.

When I told my parents about my decision to marry Stephanie, they were not happy and questioned my decision because they didn't know her as I did. They also did not think I was ready to handle the responsibility of marriage. Before I could respond in a godly way, I became angry, and my passive-aggressive behavior took over. I wanted to control how my parents felt about Stephanie, but they stopped my ability to do that. What I could do was slow down and change the way I was thinking and choose to live according to God's Word. Eventually, I did. After being married for several months, my parents visited us in Nashville. After spending time together and getting to know her better, both my father and mother loved Stephanie. The desire I had from the beginning has been fulfilled. However, there is no promise on the fulfillment of these desires.

A godly desire is any specific situation that depends on other people's cooperation, the success of events, or favorable circumstances that we have no right or ability to control. We cannot base our identity, success, or sense of worth on our desires, no matter how godly they may be, because we cannot control their fulfillment. God desires that all would repent and live (see Ezekiel 18:32), but not all will. God writes to His children so that they may not sin (see 1 John 2:1), but His sovereignty and His success are not dependent on whether or not we do.

> WE CANNOT BASE OUR IDENTITY, SUCCESS OR SENSE OF WORTH ON OUR DESIRES, NO MATTER HOW GODLY THEY MAY BE, BECAUSE WE CANNOT CONTROL THEIR FULFILLMENT.

Suppose a well-meaning pastor has a goal to triple the size of his church and win his community to Christ. Although his desire is noble, every community member can block that goal. Relentless in his pursuit, the pastor tries to manipulate the flock and pressure them to share their faith. The church will suffer a lot of pain and conflict until the pastor realizes that God's goal for him is simply to become the pastor God created him to be and that this is the best way to reach his community for Christ.

The church growth movement did well to emphasize Biblical principles of mission and evangelism, but too many pastors were left feeling like failures when their church didn't have numerical growth. The goal is to be a faithful witness and teach others to be as well. We should focus on pastoring and liberating the congregation, and then church growth will happen. What kind of witness do we have in our communities if professing Christians live defeated lives? If you help them overcome their anger, fear, anxiety, depression, lust, and other problems, you will become a disciple-making church. Offer that possibility to your community, and your church will grow.

There is nothing wrong with having godly desires such as reaching our community for Christ or having a loving, harmonious, happy family. However, we shouldn't base our identity and sense of worth on their fulfillment. We should never try to control and manipulate people to accomplish our desires, nor should we get angry, anxious, or depressed if our desires are not met—though we may feel disappointed. Life is full of disappointments, but they are likely God's appointments to greater maturity in Christ. Other people don't always cooperate, and events don't always go our way, but these realities of life do not stop us from conforming to the image of God.

The fruit (not fruits) of the Spirit is love (Galatians 5:22), which is also the goal of our instruction (1 Timothy 1:5) and the character of God (1 John 4:8). Trying to control and manipulate others to fulfill our desires (regardless of how godly they may appear) may result in character traits and emotional responses that are in direct contrast to the fruit of the Spirit.[1]

If our desires (even godly ones) aren't realized, then what is the basis for our hope? Paul answers in Romans 5:3-5 (NASB), "We also exult in our tribulations, knowing that tribulation brings about perseverance; and perseverance, proven character; and proven character, hope; and hope does not disappoint, because the love of God has been poured out within our hearts through the Holy Spirit who was given to us." Many trials and tribulations reveal wrong goals but actually make God's goal for our lives: proven character. The very thing we hope for is realized when we live by faith according to what God says is true.

Having the wrong goal may lead to faulty conclusions. This job is hopeless, therefore change jobs. This church is hopeless, therefore change churches. This marriage is hopeless, therefore change partners.

There may be legitimate times to change churches and employment, but lessons unlearned will carry over to the following location. A hopeless marriage will remain until we decide to be the spouse God created us to be and stop trying to change the other person! How much anger exhibited in our churches and homes would dissipate if we were all filled with the Holy Spirit and were committed to God's goal (will) for our lives, which is our sanctification (1 Thessalonians 4:3).

> **JESUS NEVER DISPLAYED HIS ANGER TOWARDS PEOPLE TO BREAK PEOPLE BECAUSE THEY SINNED. INSTEAD, JESUS DEMONSTRATED HIS ANGER TOWARDS SIN BECAUSE SIN LEAVES PEOPLE BROKEN.**

There is a place, however, for righteous indignation. If we wish to be angry and not sin, then be angry like Jesus was and be angry at sin. Jesus never displayed His anger towards people to break people because they sinned. Instead, Jesus demonstrated His anger towards sin because sin leaves people broken.

He turned over the tables in the temple, not the money changers. God has no blocked, uncertain, or impossible goals. We believe that righteous indignation is part of God's unchanging nature, and we think it should be part of ours, or we would never seek to correct those things that are wrong. We are called to be salt and light in a fallen world, but our awareness of what is sinful can quickly grow dull with tolerance and exposure to it. The profanity and explicit sex commonly accepted today in television and movies would have never been tolerated fifty years ago. We don't know who wrote this poetic piece, but they said it well:

> Sin is a monster of such awful mien; That to be hated, need not to be seen; But seen too oft, familiar with face; We first endure, then pity, then embrace.[2]

Learning to manage our anger when life doesn't go our way is part of the maturation process. Anger itself is not the problem. It is a God-given emotion signaling that something is wrong. So, "in your anger, do not sin; do not let the sun go down while you are still angry, and do not give the devil a foothold [literally a place]" (Ephesians 4:26,27). As soon as anger surfaces, we should separate what a goal is and what a desire is in our minds. Think of it like this: the light changed, but the car in front of you didn't budge. Of course, you desired to get through that intersection, but you are still a child of God, and such moments provide you the opportunity to live like one.

You have the God-given capacity to choose what you think and believe. You don't control your anger. You control your thoughts by taking every thought captive to the obedience of Christ (2 Corinthians 10:5). If the anger is righteous, God may guide you to pray for someone or motivate you to correct some wrong. Paul tells us to analyze the cause for our anger and deal with the aftermath before the sun sets, or we may be giving the devil grounds for harassment. It would be double jeopardy if he gave us the thought that made us angry. We can manage our emotions today by monitoring what we think and believe, but what about the emotional baggage we carry from our past?

HEALING WOUNDS AND SETTING CAPTIVES FREE

Stephanie and I met with a young African American couple in their 20s who were struggling in their marriage. They came to see us because both the husband and wife had been physically abused at a young age. They wanted to be healthy in physical intimacy, but they both had unresolved physical trauma that was triggered when they approached the subject of sex. Therefore, physical intimacy for both of them was a struggle. Whenever the wife would try to show affection towards her husband, he felt that she was too demanding, so he would physically pull away. Whenever the husband would approach his wife to try to be intimate with her, she would feel anger towards him so she would not have to be sexually intimate. When we asked them to describe their home experience from age 6 to 12, their answers were telling. She was a child of an alcoholic, and all her memories of that time in her were painful. His father left his mother when he was a young child. Unfortunately, his childhood experiences with other men in the community were riddled with physical abuse. When they came to see us, their unresolved past sexual history was wreaking havoc on their marriage.

If we talked to a group of Christians about sexual molestation, the emotional response would be anywhere from a two to a ten. The response would be around two if you have never been molested and don't know anybody who has been molested. It would be a three to an eight if you know of some people who have been molested, but your emotional response would be near ten if you had recently been molested. Have you ever had a conversation with a group of people about something, and suddenly someone responds angrily and leaves? You probably wondered, "What did I say?" Your words or attitude likely triggered a painful memory. Almost everyone has "hot buttons" that are triggered by current events.

When Stephanie and I were children, our parents let both of us watch the movie *The Exorcist*.[3] We both were traumatized by the demonic activity in that movie. Today if we see a movie preview that even looks like it could be similar to *The Exorcist*, we will turn the channel. We do not like movies that deal with the spiritual world unless it shows

Satan being defeated like in *The Passion of the Christ*.[4] Any time that movies come out about demonic possession, we wisely avoid them because we don't want to give the enemy a foothold into our lives.

People tend to avoid people, conversations, or events that trigger painful memories. *I'm not going there if he or she will be there. I stay away from movies like that. If you are going to talk about that subject, I'm leaving.* If you have had a lot of trauma in your past, your world can start shutting down. Wounds that aren't healed are transferred to others. We can try to suppress those painful memories by avoiding people and specific events, but that will only keep us bound to the past. There is one primary truth and one choice that can set us free.

> WE ARE NOT IN BONDAGE TO PAST EVENTS, BUT WE MAY BE IN BONDAGE TO THE LIES WE BELIEVED DUE TO PAST EXPERIENCES.

First, as new believers, we are not just a product of our past. We are new creations in Christ. God doesn't fix our past. He sets us free from it. We processed every experience in our past at the time it happened. Remember, we are not in bondage to past events, but we may be in bondage to the lies we believed due to past experiences. As new creations in Christ, we can reprocess those events from the perspective of being a new creation in Christ, but not as a victim. We cannot promise anyone that they won't be victimized, but we can promise them that they don't have to remain a victim anymore.

FORGIVENESS SETS US FREE

Angry people will stay that way until they forgive those who have offended them. We will inevitably suffer at the hands of others, no matter how righteously we live. Physical and emotional abuse can leave us feeling bitter, angry, and resentful. Our old nature seeks revenge and repayment, but the Spirit says, "Forgive them, just as Christ has forgiven you." But you don't know how they have hurt me! As long as we hold on to our bitterness, they are still hurting us. Forgiveness sets us free from our past and stops the pain. We don't heal in order to forgive; we forgive in order to heal.

Forgiveness is not forgetting. God says, "I will forgive their wickedness and will remember their sins no more" (Hebrews 8:12). That doesn't mean God forgets because an omniscient God couldn't forget even if He wanted to. It means that He will not use our past sins against us in the future. He will remove them as far from us as the East is from the West (see Psalm 103:12). We know that we haven't forgiven others if we continuously bring up their past and use it against them. Forgetting may be a long-term by-product of forgiving, but it is not how we forgive. Nor are we tolerating sin when we forgive others. God forgives, but He never tolerates sin. We have the right to set up Scriptural boundaries to stop future abuse.

> " WE DON'T HEAL IN ORDER TO FORGIVE; WE FORGIVE IN ORDER TO HEAL. "

Jesus forgave us by taking upon Himself the consequences of our sin. To forgive others as Christ has forgiven us means that we agree to live with the consequences of their sin. That may not seem fair, but we have to do it anyway. Everybody is living with the consequences of somebody else's sin. We are all living with the consequence of Adam's sin. The only real choice is whether we will do so in the bondage of bitterness or the freedom of forgiveness.

As long as we refuse to forgive, we are emotionally chained to past events and the people who hurt us. The purpose of forgiveness is to set a captive free, and when we do, we realize that we were the captive.

130

Bitterness is like swallowing poison and hoping the other person will die! It is for our benefit that we forgive others.

But where is the justice? The cross is what makes forgiveness morally correct. Christ died once for all our sins: his sins, her sins, our sins, and your sins. There has always been an elevation of social justice wherever Christianity flourishes. However, we will never have perfect justice in this lifetime, which is why there is a coming final judgment. The old nature wants revenge, but God said, "Do not take revenge, my dear friends, but leave room for God's wrath, for it is written: 'It is mine to avenge; I will repay,' says the Lord" (Romans 12:19). But why should we let them off our hook? That is precisely why we should forgive—because we are still hooked to them. If we let them off our hook, are they off God's hook? No. What is to be gained in forgiving others is freedom from our past. God will exact justice in the final judgment.

Forgiving others doesn't mean we refuse to testify in civil courts for the sake of social justice. Nor does it mean we avoid confronting a brother or sister living in sin. Forgiving others makes our heart right before God and allows us to experience our freedom in Christ. Only then can we righteously testify in court and confront others. If you have offended someone, don't attempt to worship God when you come under conviction (see Matthew 5:24). Go first to the person who has something against you, seek forgiveness, pay damages if necessary, and be reconciled.

If someone has offended you, don't go to that person. Go first to God and forgive that person as Christ has forgiven you. Many people wrongly think they have to go to the people who offended them in order to forgive them. That may be impossible and often is inadvisable.

The person we need to forgive may be dead or unreachable. In some cases, it would be unwise because confronting an unrepentant offender may actually set a person up for more abuse.

Jesus says we should continue forgiving as many times as necessary, "Jesus answered, 'Not seven times, Peter, but seventy times'" (Matthew 18:22). Jesus then told this parable to put our need to forgive others in perspective. The servant owed "ten thousand talents" to his master, which was way beyond a lifetime's wage (Matthew 18: 24). Repaying the debt was not possible; therefore, the servant had no choice but to ask for mercy. The master forgave him, but then the servant wouldn't forgive a fellow servant for a debt of just a hundred denarii (verse 28). A denarius was a day's wage. His master had forgiven him an enormous debt, but the man showed no mercy to a fellow servant for a much smaller debt.

God is just and can't be unjust or unrighteous for a moment. Justice is rightness or fairness. If we meted out justice, we would be giving people what they deserve. We would all be consigned to hell if God gave us what we deserved. Thankfully, God is merciful, and mercy is not giving people what they deserve. If we throw ourselves upon the mercy of the court, we are admitting to our guilt and asking for something less than what we deserve. Grace is giving to others what they don't deserve. What we have freely received we are to extend to others. We are to forgive as we have been forgiven. We are to be merciful to others as God has been merciful to us. In other words, don't give others what they deserve, but don't stop there. Give them what they don't deserve—love one another.

How do you forgive others from your heart? We have a process to forgive others in *The Steps to Freedom in Christ*. **First, we start by asking the Lord to reveal to our minds the people we need to**

forgive, including all those we have negative feelings toward. Don't overlook the need to let yourself off your own hook. Many have said that forgiving themselves was the hardest one on the list. God had already forgiven them, and there is no condemnation for those who are in Christ Jesus. In essence, they are just accepting God's forgiveness, but we have found it very helpful for them to specifically say, "Lord, I choose to forgive myself for (whatever they have done)." In many cases, we have discovered that they are being victimized by the accuser who "accuses them before God day and night" (Revelation 12:10).

Second, face the hurt and the feelings of hatred. If you are going to forgive from the heart, you have to allow the painful memories to surface. If you are unwilling to admit to the pain and the emotional damage, the forgiveness process will be incomplete. Humanly, we try to suppress our emotional pain, but God will surface names and events so we can face them and let them go. To admit that you hate your parents, for instance, means that you can now forgive them. Your feelings toward others will change only after you forgive them. What is to be gained is your freedom.

One lady worked through her list and asked for a break to visit the restroom. She had dealt with only ten offenders up to that point, but just one of those abusers would send an average person into a tailspin. When she came back and looked at the list, she said, "Why do the names on the top of the list look different to me than the remaining names?"

Before forgiveness, she couldn't mention those names without triggering painful memories. They no longer had any hold on her. That is what freedom brings.

Third, forgiveness is a crisis of the will. You choose to bear the consequences of the person's sin. You choose to let go of the past and grab hold of God. You choose not to seek revenge. Don't wait until you feel like forgiving because you will never get there. God is not asking you to like the person who offended you; He is asking you to forgive as you have been forgiven so He can set you free and heal your damaged emotions. Let Him be the avenger. Stop the pain by forgiving from your heart every person who has offended you for every offensive thing he or she did. You can do this by praying (preferably out loud), "Lord, I choose to forgive [person] for [verbally expressing every hurt and pain the Lord brings to your mind and how it made you feel]."

Fourth, after you have forgiven every person for every painful memory: Finish by praying,

> Lord, I release all these people to You, and I release my right
> to seek revenge. I choose not to hold on to my bitterness
> and anger, and I ask You to heal my damaged emotions.
> In Jesus' name, I pray. Amen.

After many years of leading many people through *The Steps to Freedom*, we can say without qualification that forgiving others is the biggest issue confronting believers. The average person will have twenty to thirty names surface when they pray. Forgiving another person from our heart is the most Christ-like decision we will ever make. The *Freedom in Christ Course* has an entire lesson on forgiveness. When Neil taught at the first conference we attended, he prayed, asking God on behalf of everyone attending to bring to our minds those people we needed to forgive. He waited a couple of minutes and then said, "I am not going to embarrass anyone, but I sense the need to give you an opportunity to respond to God. If you know there are one or more people you need to forgive and are willing to do that, would you stand right now? I will not ask for anything more than that, but in standing, you are saying, *God, I hear you, and I am willing to forgive, and I need your grace to do that.*" Stephanie and I immediately stood to our feet and noticed that nearly everyone else was standing as well. We all were given the opportunity to choose to walk in forgiveness.

When we take people through *The Steps*, we ask them to pray and ask the Lord to reveal to their minds who they need to forgive. If our ministry is reconciliation and we want to be a disciple-making church, we have to teach our people how to forgive others and give them regular opportunities to practice it.

CHAPTER 7

Overcoming Anxiety Disorders

D r. Edmund Bourne is the author of *The Anxiety and Phobia Workbook*,[1] which won the Benjamin Franklin Book Award for Excellence in Psychology. Dr. Bourne entered this field of study because he struggled with anxiety. Five years after the publication of the first edition, his anxiety disorder took a turn for the worse, causing him to reevaluate his own life and his approach to treatment. Then he published a new book entitled *Healing Fear*. In the foreword, he wrote:[2]

> The guiding metaphor for this book is "healing," as an approach to overcoming anxiety, in contrast to "applied technology." I feel it's important to introduce this perspective into the field of anxiety treatment since the vast majority of self-help books available (including my first book) utilize the applied technology approach.
>
> I don't want to diminish the importance of cognitive-behavioral therapy (CBT) and the applied technology approach. Such an approach produces effective results

in many cases, and I use it in my professional practice every day. In the past few years, though, I feel that the cognitive-behavioral strategy has reached its limits. CBT and medication can produce results quickly and are very compatible with the short-term therapy, managed-care environment in the mental health profession at present. When follow-up is done over one- to three-year intervals, however, some of the gains are lost. Relapses occur rather often, and people seem to get themselves back into the same difficulties that precipitated the original anxiety disorder.

In other words, "They have healed the brokenness of My people superficially, saying, 'Peace, peace,' when there is no peace" (Jeremiah 6:14 NASB).

Before we get too proud about our successes of applying the Gospel with "effective results," we too must acknowledge that many will fall back into their old flesh patterns unless they genuinely repent. We mentioned earlier that CBT is compatible with repentance but will fall far short if it does not include God and overlooks the spiritual world's reality. We don't know whether Dr. Bourne has a saving knowledge of the Lord Jesus Christ. Still, in his research, he came to the following conclusion: "In my own experience, spirituality has been important, and I believe it will come to play an increasingly important role in the psychology of the future."[3] We hope he is correct, but not every new emphasis on spirituality will be Biblically based.

ANXIETY

Anxiety is like fear but without an adequate cause. People are anxious because they don't know what will happen next. The word anxiety occurs about twenty-five times in the New Testament. Sometimes it is used in the positive sense of caring. People are considered mentally healthy if they are relatively free from anxiety. Whenever Stephanie and I are getting ready to speak at a church, seminar or marriage conference, we feel anxious, as we should. The proper response is for us to study, prepare, and allow the Holy Spirit to speak through us, with the help of our preparation. In light of the racial injustice in America and how people of color have been treated in this country, anytime our children travel across the country on tour, we become anxious. We are not sure how they will be treated if authorities stop them. We feel a real sense of anxiety because of our own experiences. Although we feel anxious, our first response to anxiety is prayer.

Jesus' discourse on anxiety in the Sermon on the Mount begins by questioning what we treasure, and in whom we trust: "Do not store up for yourselves treasures on earth, where moths and rust destroy, and where thieves break in and steal. But store up treasures in heaven" (Matthew 6:19, 20 CSB). Treasures on earth have two characteristics. According to the thermodynamic laws, all systems become increasingly disorderly and eventually decay. Therefore, constant care is necessary to maintain all earthly treasures. Second, there will always be thieves who covet what others have; therefore, treasures must be kept secure. It is hard to be anxiety-free while worrying about our earthly possessions, which we can't take with us.

> **❝ ANXIOUS PEOPLE LOVE THINGS AND USE PEOPLE. PEACEMAKERS USE THINGS TO LOVE PEOPLE. ❞**

On the other hand, storing up treasures in heaven is profitable for this age and the one to come. "For where your treasure is, there your heart will be also" (vs. 21 CSB). Anxious people love things and use people. Peacemakers use things to love people. Peaceful existence and a sense of security come from eternal relationships, not material possessions.

Jesus continues, "The eye is the lamp of the body. If your eyes are healthy, your whole body will be full of light. But if your eyes are unhealthy, your whole body will be full of darkness" (vs. 22,23 NIV). Ancient tradition viewed the eyes as the window through which light enters the body. If the eyes were in good condition, the whole body would receive the benefits that light bestows. If bad, the entire body would be plunged into darkness, breeding disease. There is a subtle nuance in this passage that is pregnant with meaning. The "clear eye" is the one with a single vision, which Jesus clarifies in the next verse. "No one can serve two masters. Either you will hate the one and love the other, or you will be devoted to one and despise the other. You cannot serve God and money" (vs. 24).

Anxiety (*merimna*, Greek) is a combination of *merizo*, which means divide, and nous, which means mind. In other words, an anxious person is double-minded, and, according to James, a double-minded person is unstable in all their ways (James 1:8). The King James translation picked up that idea in the next verse, "Therefore I say unto you, take no thought for ("do not be worried about," NASB) your life" (Matthew 6:25). Jesus is saying, *Trust Me. I take care of the birds in the air and the lilies of the field, and you are worth far more to Me than animals and plants. I know you need food, clothing, and shelter. If you seek first the kingdom of God and His righteousness, all these things will be added to you* (Matthew 6:26-33).

CASTING YOUR ANXIETY UPON CHRIST

When the world saw the gruesome murder of George Floyd, it opened the eyes of many to see what the African American community had been expressing for generations. There is very little trust in the African

American community regarding how police have treated people of color in the United States. Many African Americans are afraid of what they will experience in their next police encounter. The US Census Bureau data found that anxiety among African Americans has increased by 26%.[4] Hopefully, through much-needed conversation and reform, change is on the way. What are some Biblical and psychological strategies to help individuals resolve this and other forms of anxiety so that they can have better mental health?

First, turn to God in prayer. Paul wrote, "Do not be anxious for anything, but in every situation, by prayer and, with thanksgiving, present your requests to God" (Philippians 4:6 CSB). In other words, don't be double-minded about anything. The first thing Christians should do about anything is pray.

Second, resolve all personal and spiritual conflicts. We know we sound redundant, but we firmly believe the answer lies in submitting to God and resisting the devil. If you have thoroughly gone through *The Steps to Freedom in Christ*, there is no need to keep resolving the same old issue. We regularly lead people through *The Steps*, which helps us stay in touch with hurting humanity, but we also get a personal house cleaning every time we do it. Consider the context for Peter's instruction to cast our anxiety on Christ: "Humble yourselves, therefore under God's mighty hand, that he may lift you up in due time. Cast all your anxiety on him because he cares for you. Be alert and of a sober mind. Your enemy, the devil, prowls around like a roaring lion, looking for someone to devour. Resist him, standing firm in the faith" (1 Peter 5:6-9). If a believer is paying attention to a deceiving spirit, they are double-minded and therefore anxious.

Third, state the problem. People can't see the forest for the trees in an anxious state of mind. Many anxious people find relief by simply having their situation clarified and put into perspective. A problem well stated is half solved. Generally speaking, the process of worrying takes a more significant toll on a person than the negative consequences of what they are worried about. As African American parents, there is no worst-case scenario than to hear that our children have gotten pulled over by the police, especially a son. Thank God we have not had any harmful incidents. However, it does not stop us from feeling anxious. If something were to happen (God forbid), we could take matters into our own hands by acting out of anger, bitterness, or vengeance, which are only temporary solutions. No one can take care of your mental, emotional and spiritual well-being like Jesus.

Fourth, divide the facts from the assumptions. People may be fearful of the facts but not necessarily anxious. Anxious people don't know what is going to happen tomorrow. Since we don't know, we make assumptions, and the natural tendency is to assume the worst. Not every police officer is a bad officer, and not every African American is a danger to society. If the assumption is not based on truth, then what you feel will not be based on reality. Those who act upon unsubstantiated assumptions will likely regret doing so.

Fifth, determine what you have the right and ability to control. You are only responsible for what you have the right and the ability to control. You are not responsible for that which you don't. Your sense of worth is tied to what you will be held accountable for. If you are living an irresponsible life, you should feel anxious. Don't try to cast your responsibility onto Christ. He will throw it back. However, do cast your anxiety onto Him if you are living a responsible life because His integrity is at stake in meeting your needs.

Sixth, list everything that you can do related to the situation that is your responsibility. Then commit yourself to be a responsible person and fulfill your calling and obligations in life. At this point, you have done the best you can, and that is all God is asking. Any residual anxiety is probably due to your assuming responsibilities that God never intended you to have.

> " IF THE ASSUMPTION IS NOT BASED ON TRUTH, THEN WHAT YOU FEEL WILL NOT BE BASED ON REALITY. "

PANIC ATTACKS

Panic attacks (sometimes referred to as anxiety attacks) are defined as "very frightening and aversive experiences in which people are overwhelmed with the physical symptoms of anxiety."[5] Panic disorder is twice as common in women as in men.[6]

After suffering several panic episodes, many become increasingly afraid that they are helpless victims. There are approximately 6 million Americans who suffer panic attacks, but that condition, if not resolved, will eventually develop into agoraphobia, which claims millions of victims.[7] Since they don't know when an attack may happen, they become fearful of going to public events where such an episode would be highly embarrassing. If they manage to attend church, they will likely sit in the back row or near an exit.

There is no physical enemy to fight or flee from during a panic attack, and yet the body responds as though there is. Symptoms include almost paralyzing terror, racing heartbeat, nausea, lightheadedness, chest pains, sudden chills, and feeling as though you can't get enough air. In a genuine emergency, our breathing undergoes a significant change in rate and pattern, which also happens during a panic attack.

The initial physical response to a real or imagined fear object is to gasp or suck in air. Then instead of exhaling, we try to suck in more air, but there is no room for it in the lungs. Having people blow into a paper bag gets them to exhale and return to normal breathing. Knowing that most of the unpleasant physical symptoms of panic attacks are the body's God-created means of coping with a perceived emergency takes a lot of the terrifying mystery out of these episodes. What initially seems to be an overwhelming situation becomes much more manageable if we understand what our bodies naturally do.

Suppose you develop a minor condition, say fibroid tumors and polyps in your ovaries, common in African American women but usually benign or non-cancerous. Your first experience could be frightening because you don't know what it is, and it may seem life-threatening. After a thorough physical exam, you learn that it is only a minor condition that can be removed. The next time you feel a little overwhelmed from an overactive menstrual cycle, your renewed mind interprets the data differently, and there is no (or less) panic. The first episode would be less frightening if your mind was previously programmed not to fear death. Other physical conditions may result in panic attacks, so a thorough physical exam should always be considered an option for treatment.

There are spiritual mysteries surrounding panic attacks that medicine and secular psychology cannot address. What causes a person who usually can handle stress to become stricken with a panic attack suddenly? Why do they call it an anxiety attack when it feels much more like fear? Is it because they cannot identify the fear object; therefore, it better fits the definition of anxiety? Why do people suddenly awaken terrorized from a sound sleep? Why do Christians often find instantaneous freedom from these attacks when they call upon the name of the Lord? These questions were likely on the mind of someone who contacted our ministry:

I wonder if you can help me out with a particular experience that has plagued me and my sleep for the past six or seven years. Although I am a Christian, I have probably experienced about 15 of these panic attacks over the past several years. They are usually associated with a time in which I've given something over to God or committed my ways to Him.

Here is a little history of my sleeping habits. When I was young, I would dream very intense dreams about spirits or things related to the spiritual world. I'm not sure why, except that I am an artist and have a very vivid imagination. Other nights I would have intense dreams about the end times!

As I got older, these dreams would happen less frequently, but they came with the same intensity when they did come. When I turned 17, I received a very distinct call from God. Unfortunately, I did not follow that calling because of my pride and fear. Since then, I have received many opportunities to pursue that original calling, and each time I would have a panic attack. Consequently, I didn't respond to the call because I feared another attack.

The panic attack usually starts by waking me out of my sleep to either a rushing sound in my ear, many people talking incoherently, or screaming. After about five or ten seconds, an intense, indescribable fear envelops my whole body.

I feel physically paralyzed, and I can't say anything, but I can move my eyes around and hear. It feels like there is a heavyweight resting on my chest, pushing me into my bed. This whole experience lasts about a minute, but I am usually wide awake and scared. I'm not sure what causes this, but I think it may be demonic.[8]

The fact that the attacks occurred when she was making serious moves toward God indicates a spiritual attack. Unfortunately, the scare tactic worked. The fear of something other than God kept her from following Him, which is a very common strategy of Satan. The kind of attack she described would happen to Neil every night before he began a *"Resolving Personal and Spiritual Conflicts"* conference, and it continued for four years. I (Daryl) also experienced several such attacks. We have learned how to stand against such an attack and fall back to sleep within minutes.

We have asked conference attendees two questions. First, "How many of you have been sharply awakened at a precise time like 3:00 a.m.?" At least a third of the people raised their hands. The people we have helped come out of satanism reported that 3:00 a.m. is the culmination of satanic rituals. Satanists pray for our demise and attempt to summon and send demons to attack believers. It is no sin to be under attack, and believers should know, "You, dear children, are from God and have overcome them because the one who is in you is greater than the one who is in the world" (1 John 4:4; see also 1 John 5:18). It is only an annoyance for a person of faith.

Second, "How many have been suddenly overwhelmed with fear at night? You probably felt half asleep and half awake. It could feel as though something was pushing on your chest or grabbing your throat.

You tried to move or say something, but you couldn't." Again, at least a third of the people raised their hands. If we call upon the name of the Lord, we shall be saved, but what if we can't physically do that? The fear object is not physical, so it can't be resolved physically. "For though we live in the world, we do not wage war as the world does. The weapons we fight with are not the weapons of the world. On the contrary, they have divine power to demolish strongholds" (2 Corinthians 10:3, 4). God knows the thoughts and intentions of our hearts, so we can mentally submit ourselves to God and call upon the Lord in our minds. The moment we do, we will be able to speak. Then all we would have to say is "Jesus," and the devil will flee. It needs to be said aloud because Satan is under no obligation to obey our thoughts, which he doesn't perfectly know. You don't have to scream! Just verbally whispering or speaking calmly works. The order of Scripture is critical. We must first submit to God inwardly, and then we will be able to resist the devil outwardly (see James 4:7).

Spiritual attacks usually occur at night when we are alone and vulnerable. Being awakened out of a sound sleep heightens our sense of terror because we are caught off guard and easily confused. There are many references in Scripture where humans are overwhelmed with fear in the presence of angelic beings. Job's friend, Eliphaz, described an experience he had:

> Now a word was brought to me stealthily, and my ear received a whisper of it. Amid disquieting thoughts from the visions of the night, when deep sleep falls on men, dread came upon me, and trembling, and made all my bones shake. Then a spirit passed by my face; the hair of my flesh bristled up. It stood still, but I could not discern its appearance; a form was before my eyes (Job 4:12-16, NASB).

Notice that he said, "a spirit," not the Spirit. Such demonic visitations are seldom explained in our churches, which leaves believers unequipped and often shaken to the core. Only the Church can provide adequate answers for the anxiety disorders plaguing the planet. A congregation that is paralyzed by fear has lost its witness. "The wicked flee when no one is pursuing, but the righteous are bold as a lion" (Proverbs 28:1 NASB). That was not the case for the early Church. "And when they had prayed, the place where they had gathered together was shaken, and they were all filled with the Holy Spirit and began to speak the word of God with boldness" (Acts 4:31 NASB). Being courageous is the mark of Spirit-filled believers. We gather together as believers to encourage one another. Encouragement from others emboldens us to step out in faith and not in fear.

FEAR

Fear is the most basic instinct of every living creature. Anxiety disorders include fear, anxiety, and panic attacks. An animal without fear will become some predator's dinner. Fear is a God-given natural response to anything that threatens our physical safety and psychological well-being. Rational fears are learned and vital for our survival. Falling off a chair at an early age helps us develop a healthy respect for heights. Touching a hot stove teaches us to stay away from other items that will burn us. Phobias are irrational fears that compel us to do irresponsible things or keep us from doing what we should. The key to overcoming any phobia is identifying the lie behind its irrationality, which is another confirmation that truth sets us free.

Fear is different from anxiety and panic attacks because fear has an object. Fears or phobias are categorized by their objects. Acrophobia is a fear of high places. Claustrophobia is a fear of enclosed places.

Agoraphobia is a generalized fear of public settings; *agora* is the Greek word for marketplace. For a fear object to be effective, it must be perceived by humans or animals as having two attributes. It must be imminent (present) and potent (possessing some power that can negatively affect us).

We have a reasonably healthy fear of rattlesnakes. However, we have no fear of them as we write this chapter because there are none present. If one slithered through the door and coiled under our chairs unnoticed, we would still sense no fear because we have no awareness of its presence. However, our fear index would go from zero to ten immediately upon seeing it at our feet. If you threw a dead rattlesnake at our feet (provided we were sure that it was dead), we wouldn't fear it. Remove just one of those two attributes, and the fear dissipates.

It is essential to recognize the learned aspect of fear objects. For instance, when we lived in our first house in East Nashville, I happened to see an entire family of snakes slithering along in the grass while mowing our backyard. I immediately wanted to know what type of snakes they were. I found out from my neighbor they were harmless garden snakes. Suppose my son is playing in the backyard and sees a small one crawling across the grass. Because my son loves nature and loves playing outside, he will likely pick it up. The average mother (my wife) would probably freak out. Because I know that the snake is harmless, I would not be as fearful of the snake. Total ignorance is dangerous. Partial or incorrect knowledge can be paralyzing, but there is complete freedom in knowing the truth. Most fears are subsets of three major fear objects: death, people, and Satan. For instance, the fear of death is the likely root of claustrophobia (suffocating to death)

and acrophobia (dying from a fall). We can overcome all irrational fears by knowing the truth and by knowing that God has removed one of the attributes for the three major fear objects.

Physical death is imminent, "Just as people are destined to die once and after that to face judgment" (Hebrews 9:27), but it is no longer potent because of the resurrection of Jesus. "Death has been swallowed up in victory, 'Where O death, is your victory? Where O death, is your sting" (1 Corinthians 15:54, 55?) Jesus said, "I am the resurrection and the life. The one who believes in me will live [spiritually] even though they die [physically], and whoever lives by believing in me will never die [spiritually]" (John 11:25, 26). Every born-again believer can say with Paul, "For to me, to live is Christ and to die is gain" (Philippians 1:21). Many people believe that dying is the worst thing that can happen to them, but Paul says otherwise. Absence from the body is to be present with the Lord in a resurrected body that has no pain. The ultimate value is being in union with God, not with our body, which someday we will all separate from. James Elliot, the martyred missionary, wrote, "He is no fool to give up that which he cannot keep in order to gain that which he cannot lose."[9] Knowing this truth is not a license to commit suicide because it is required that we be good stewards of the physical life God has entrusted to us. However, the person who is free from the fear of death is free to live today.

Fear rooted in other people includes rejection, failure, abandonment, and even death. Jesus said, "Do not be afraid of those who kill the body but cannot kill the soul. Rather be afraid of the one who can destroy both soul, and body in hell" (Matthew 10:28). Peter wrote, "But even if you should suffer for what is right, you are blessed. Do not fear their threats; do not be frightened. But in your hearts, revere Christ as Lord. Always be prepared to give an answer to everyone

who asks you to give the reason for the hope that you have. But do this with gentleness and respect" (1 Peter 3: 14,15; see also Proverbs 29:25). The primary reason Christians don't share their faith is the fear of people or, more specifically, the fear of rejection and failure. Is it rational to let those fears keep others from hearing the good news?

Why is the fear of God the beginning of wisdom (Proverbs 9:10)? How can that fear overcome all other fears? God is the ultimate fear object because He is omnipresent and omnipotent. When we worship God, we are ascribing to Him His divine attributes. The Father seeks those who do that in spirit and in truth (John 4:23). This is not because He needs us to tell Him who He is; it is for our benefit that we worship God. By doing so we keep His divine attributes fresh in our minds. Isaiah wrote: "You are not to say, 'It is a conspiracy!' in regard to all that these people call a conspiracy, and you are not to fear what they fear or be in dread of it. It is the Lord of Hosts whom you should regard as Holy. And He shall be your fear, and He shall be your dread. Then He shall become a sanctuary" (8:12,13, NASB). Spirit-filled Christians who know the truth have found their sanctuary in Christ. They are the true worshipers that God is seeking.

God rules supreme over every other fear object – including Satan. Even though "Your enemy, the devil, prowls about like a roaring lion, looking for someone to devour" (1 Peter 5:8), he has been disarmed (imminent, but not potent). Jesus came to destroy the works of the devil (1 John 3:8). "And having disarmed the powers and authorities, He made a public spectacle of them, triumphing over them by the cross" (Colossians 2:15). Most people in churches fear Satan more than they fear God. In doing so, they elevate Satan as a greater object of worship.

OVERCOMING IRRATIONAL FEARS

Overcoming conflicts begins by reconciling with God. David wrote, "I sought the Lord and He answered me and delivered me from all my fears. ...The angel of the Lord encamps around those who fear Him, and He delivers them" (Psalms 34:4,7). That is why we always start with *The Steps to Freedom in Christ*. The research shared in Chapter Four reveals that many fears are overcome by resolving personal and spiritual conflicts, i.e., by seeking first the Kingdom of God. Because flesh patterns remain, not all fears are easily overcome. If you don't reconcile with God, it becomes more difficult to cope, and life becomes hard to manage, as illustrated by the following story:

There was a very sweet girl looking for some spiritual direction, and I (Stephanie) desired to pour into her life. Although I did not know her well, I could see that she was in a battle. One of the ways we walk with people is to take them through a study of the book *Victory Over the Darkness* for eight weeks. It has proven to be a very effective discipleship tool when those we walk with put in the time to do the work. As I began to walk with her, it was evident that she was dealing with many unresolved emotional and spiritual issues from her past. Her mom died when she was very young. She was sexually molested at a very young age. She was in and out of the foster care system.

She has no siblings or close relatives except a beautiful daughter who was suffering because of her mother's fears. She has developed a lot of fear and trust issues, which is understandable. She seems to be making progress when she chooses to put in the work, but it appears that any event that she goes through triggers irrational and sometimes paralyzing fears. She is in real bondage! She has seen several counselors and has been on and off medication. I am hopeful because we serve the God of hope. She can be helped because Jesus died for her sins and desires for her to be free from all of her personal and spiritual conflicts. However, if she continues to live her life independently of God and follow deceiving spirits, it is not hard to see that she will lose control. I walk with her and encourage her to seek a balance of Biblical counseling and help from a psychiatrist who has a Biblical worldview. Unfortunately, if she does not repent from her unresolved conflicts, submit to God, and resist the devil, she will go deeper and deeper into spiritual bondage.

That which has been learned must be unlearned. After we have led inquirers through *The Steps*, we use the following approach to overcome any residual fears:

First, start by analyzing your fears. What are you afraid of? What event precipitated your first experience of that fear? There is always a cause and an effect. Ask God to reveal that to you. What is the root lie that makes the fear irrational? Which of the two attributes of the fear object can be eliminated?

Second, analyze your lifestyle. Fear is a powerful motivator for good and evil. How has fear prevented you from living a responsible life, compelled you to do that which is irresponsible, or led you to compromise your witness? A timid Christian homemaker who fears her pagan husband will likely compromise her witness through irresponsible behavior. An intimidated employee may lie for his or her boss even though he or she knows it is wrong. Students may succumb to peer pressure and compromise their faith because they fear that their friends will reject them.

Third, decide on a responsible plan of action. So far, you have submitted to God, resisted the devil, and identified your fears and the lies behind them. Hopefully, you now understand how anxiety is negatively affecting your behavior. The next step is to face the fear and prayerfully work out a realistic plan to overcome it. For instance, if you are afraid to ride an elevator, choose a two-story building, enter the elevator and come out before the door closes. Then open the door and let it close on you. Then open it again. Finally, go in and push the second-floor button. Have a friend ride with you if necessary. Don't start by going to the Empire State Building and pushing the top floor button! Evangelism Explosion is successful because it helps trainees overcome their fears by going with an experienced trainer and observing. Then they are encouraged to participate with the trainer, and the final step is to take the lead while the trainer observes.

Fourth, if the fear object is a person, determine in advance how you will respond to their possible reactions to your plan. How should you respond if they ignore you, get mad at you, or threaten harm when you no longer let them control your life?

Fifth, commit yourself to carry out the plan in the power of the Holy Spirit. Do the thing you fear the most, and the death of fear is certain. There is no other way to overcome fearful flesh patterns. We want the fear to go away first so we can live responsibly, but it is the other way around.

The first time I sat under Neil's teaching, I (Daryl) finally heard an explanation for my night terrors. I felt empowered after learning my identity and position in Christ. I realized that all authority had been given to Jesus, and Jesus commissioned us to go and make disciples with His authority and power. "The One Who is in you is greater than the one who is in the world" (1 John 4:4). Knowing that for myself was liberating, but I still struggled with the fear of helping others resolve their issues.

When Neil asked me to sit in as a prayer partner in a *Steps* appointment, I gladly accepted. That was the catalyst that led to hundreds of other freedom appointments. Now we invite others to sit in with us as prayer partners, but they are also there to learn and be equipped to help others.

FEAR OF FAILURE

While preparing to film the *Freedom in Christ Course*, the possibility of failing was my primary fear. I had never been asked to be a part of a 10-week long discipleship course before, much less have an audience and a whole film crew that would be there watching me. I was not sure I could complete such a huge task. It seemed like my wife had to encourage me every step of the way. I did not want to fail! There were hours upon hours of preparation time that my wife and I had to put in to get ready to film the discipleship course. It will probably not surprise you to know that the fear of failure is a universal problem plaguing many people. Trying not to fail actually distracts us from succeeding. Allowing any fear object other than God to control us prevents us from living by faith in God. We believe there are three principles of success that are not dependent upon other people or circumstances.

First, to be successful, we need to know God and His ways. The Israelites were liberated from Egypt but were about to face some giants in the Promised Land. Joshua wrote, "Be strong and very courageous; be careful to obey all the law which my servant Moses gave you; do not turn from it to the right or to the left, that you may be successful wherever you go" (Joshua 1:7). Paul wrote, "I consider everything a loss because of the surpassing worth of knowing Christ Jesus my Lord" (Philippians 3:8).

Second, to be successful, we must choose to believe and live according to the person God has called us to be (Philippians 3:12-14). We would be more successful as Christians if we put character before career, maturity before ministry, and being before doing.

Third, to be successful, we must be good stewards of the time, talent, and treasure God has entrusted to us (1 Corinthians 4:1,2). Nobody can keep us from following those three principles. Successful Christians play for the "Coach" and not the grandstand.

Knowing what failure is *not* is just as important as knowing what constitutes success. To stumble and fall is not failure. I stumbled more than a few times when filming, but that is what good editors are for. "For though the righteous fall seven times, they rise again" (Proverbs 24:16). In the end, with the help of my wonderful wife, Steve Goss (our International Director), and the production team, I think we did a pretty good job! You can purchase the curriculum for yourself to see the finished product! Again, to stumble and fall is not failure. Failure comes when you don't take responsibility for your stumble or fall. A mistake is never a failure unless you fail to learn from it. A young executive was about to replace a highly successful Chief Executive Officer. He asked the CEO, "Sir, how do you account for your incredible success?" He sternly said, "No mistakes." The young man responded, "But, sir, how do you get to the point where you make no mistakes?" To which he replied, "A lot of experience." "What kind of experience do you mean?" the young executive asked. "A lot of mistakes," answered the wise old man.

CHAPTER 8

Overcoming Depression

Dearest,

I feel certain I am going mad again. I feel we can't go through another of those terrible times. And I shan't recover this time. I begin to hear voices, and I can't concentrate. So, I am doing what seems the best thing to do. You have given me the greatest possible happiness. You have been in every way all that anyone could be. I don't think two people could have been happier till this terrible disease came. I can't fight any longer.[1]

This is the opening scene in *The Hours*, a book and movie that draws on the life and work of Virginia Woolf. *The Hours* intertwines three stories of severely depressed people. This was the suicide note that Virginia Woolf penned for her husband before she drowned herself in a river. The title is in reference to the hours and hours of never-ending agony that accompany depression. Her present circumstances were anything but negative, so why was she depressed? And what are those "voices?"

According to the National Institute of Mental Health, approximately 8 percent of all adults in the United States struggled with depression in 2019. Research shows that less than half of those people will actually seek treatment for their depression, so the actual number could be much higher.[2] And we're not even including the toll of the COVID-19 pandemic on people's mental health. Even King David had a whole heart for God, yet his numerous bouts of depression are recorded throughout the Psalms. I would not be shocked to find out that Dr. Martin Luther King Jr. struggled with depression. The constant struggles he faced for freedom and justice, and the setbacks, arrests, and death threats he and his family endured would take their toll on anyone. The Bible says, "hope deferred makes the heart sick" (see Proverbs 13:12). Abraham Lincoln said, "I am now the most miserable man living. If what I feel were equally distributed to the whole human family, there would not be one cheerful face on the earth."[3] Friends of Abraham Lincoln said, "He was a sad-looking man; his melancholy dript from him as he walked,"[4] and "He was so overcome with mental depression that he never dared carry a knife in his pocket."[5]

Janet Jackson, the sister of famous artist Michael Jackson, told the Washington Post she struggled with depression throughout her early career and made the mistake of not reaching out for help." She also said, "*Looking back on it now, it was depression. But it hits a lot of people—and a lot of artists, and I didn't know that. Nobody ever talked about that in my family—I still haven't talked to anybody in my family about it.*"[6] People in the African American community are more likely than the general population to misunderstand mental illness, yet they are 20% more likely to experience serious mental illness, according the Anxiety & Depression Association of America.[7] Depression is often seen as a personal weakness or a form of punishment. Many African Americans are reluctant to discuss mental health issues and seek treatment because of the shame and stigma associated with mental illness. An older African American man wrote the following letter after he asked for help with his depression:

As Pastor Daryl began the session, I had no pretense or expectation of what was about to happen. For years I believe that God has been talking to me and that I was not getting it or not listening. During the session, I believe I heard God say, "Love others as I have loved you." I am not an emotional, sensitive, or overly spiritual person, so I knew it must have been God when the words came to me. I simply don't think about how I love people or have relationships with others. I have believed that expressing my feelings is overrated, and doing so causes one to lose focus. I have thought that emotional connections make individuals weak and unreliable and cause poor decision-making. Now I believe that I must engage in a more meaningful, thoughtful, and spiritual way with my wife and others. This is not a comfortable position for me. The relationships I have had were superficial and easier to manage. Now I realize that the devil wants me to be alone and disconnected from others to influence my thoughts and actions better. I have asked the Lord to help me with the Freedom In Christ message and my life application. I am not sure how to love others or connect in a meaningful way. I will do my best to be more engaged and open to emotional connections with my wife, family, and friends. I am under no false pretense that this will be an easy change, and I will make mistakes or slip back into my old way of thinking. However, I believe that God will lead me and guide me if I am willing, and I am.

The Christian community is generally good at meeting physical needs. When someone breaks their leg, people bring meals, do housework, and sign the cast. But when someone struggles with mental and emotional issues, the need goes largely unmet. When prayer requests are solicited at church, seldom does anyone say they are struggling with an anxiety disorder, depression, or anger. The lack of emotional honesty has resulted in many suffering needlessly.

> **DEPRESSION IS A NATURAL RESULT WHEN WE EXPERIENCE LOSS IN OUR LIVES.**

Living in this fallen world can be depressing. Depression is a natural result when we experience loss in our lives. It is critically important that we understand how to respond to such losses since everything we now possess, we shall someday lose. God intends that we grow through the trials of life and learn how to overcome feelings of helplessness and hopelessness. The richest treasures are often discovered in the deepest holes. We need the assurance that can only comes from our God of all hope.

PHYSICAL SYMPTOMS OF DEPRESSION[8]

Energy Level: *I just don't feel like doing anything.*
Lack of energy, excessive fatigue, and unrelenting tiredness are melancholy characteristics. Walking, talking, cleaning the house, getting ready for work, or doing a project can take considerably longer than usual. The lowered energy level and lowered interest in activities affects job performance. The severely depressed don't groom themselves or get dressed and either stay in bed or lie around the house.

Sleep Disturbance: *I didn't sleep again last night!*
Having trouble sleeping is one of the most common symptoms of depression. Although some people feel like sleeping all of the time, it
160

is more common to hear about insomnia. Initial insomnia (sleep-onset insomnia) is the difficulty in falling asleep, which is more likely for those struggling with anxiety disorders. Depression is more commonly associated with terminal insomnia. People fall asleep out of sheer fatigue but then wake up and can't get back to sleep. The inability to sleep contributes to the downward spiral of depression and leaves the sufferer with less energy for the next day.

Activity level: *Whatever!*

Depression is accompanied by a decreased involvement in meaningful activities, a lack of interest in life, and a lack of commitment to follow through. Many find it difficult to pray because God seems like a distant figure.

Lack of sex drive: *Not tonight!*

Accompanying this loss of desire for sex is a wish for isolation, feelings of worthlessness, criticism of one's appearance, loss of spontaneity, and apathy. The emotional state of depression usually creates problems in relationships, further curtailing the desire to be intimate.

Somatic complaints: *I ache all over!*

Many depressed people report physical aches and pains such as headaches, stomachache, and lower back pain, which can be pretty severe. In a state of depression, David wrote, "I am bowed down and brought very low; all day long I go about mourning. My back is filled with searing pain; there is no health in my body" (Psalm 38:6-7).

Loss of Appetite: *I'm not hungry!*

A decrease in appetite often accompanies depression. However, in 20% of the cases, there is an increase in appetite and craving for comfort food.

MENTAL AND EMOTIONAL SYMPTOMS OF DEPRESSION

The most commonly known symptoms of depression are emotional. There are also resultant mental states that indicate severe to mild depression, but keep in mind that what a person thinks or believes is also a cause for depression. The following are the most common emotional symptoms and mental states of those who are depressed:

Sadness: *I feel awful!*
Depression is most often characterized by profound sadness. The "blues" seem to creep up slowly, accompanied by a spirit of heaviness. Crying and brooding are common for those who are in a funk.

Despair: *It doesn't matter!*
Despair is the absence of hope. Despair sees no light at the end of the tunnel, no hope at the end of the day, and no answers for the endless round of questions that plague the mind of the depressed. Three times the Psalmists cried out, "Why my soul, are you in downcast? And why so disturbed within me? Put your hope in God, for I will yet praise him, my Savior and my God" (Psalm 42:11; 43:5).

Irritability and low frustration tolerance: *I'm done with you!*
Depressed people have very little emotional reserve. Small things tick them off, and they are easily frustrated. They have a low tolerance level for the pressures of life.

Isolation and withdrawal: *I'm going to my room!*
People who suffer with depression pull away from others. They feel embarrassed to be with people when they feel so low. They don't want to be a wet blanket in the group and drag the others down by

their depression. Although some may think that isolation is a viable short-term solution, avoidance often adds to the downward spiral of depression.

Negative thought patterns: *I can't do anything right!*
Depressed people generally have a negative view of themselves, their present circumstances, and the future. Such beliefs are more the cause than the symptom.

Thoughts of suicide: *Everybody would be better off if I just died!*
Sadness, isolation, loss of energy, strained relationships, and physical problems contaminate one's perspective of self and the future. Believing themselves to be helpless and hopeless, many begin to think of suicide as the only way out. Depression is a leading cause of suicide for teenagers and adults.

STEPS TO OVERCOMING DEPRESSION[9]

Recovery begins by saying, "I have a problem, and I need help." There are adequate answers for depression, but you have to want to get well and be willing to do whatever it takes to do it. The key to any cure is commitment. We offer the following sequential order for overcoming depression.

First: Submit to God and resist the devil (Matthew 6:33; James 4:7).
God can do wonders with a broken heart if you give Him all the pieces. In our Western world, we have been conditioned to seek every possible natural explanation and cure first. When that is not successful, *then there is nothing more that we can do but pray.* Scripture has a different order: "But seek first his kingdom and his righteousness, and all these things will be given to you as well" (Matthew 6:33). The first thing a

Christian should do about anything is pray, which we do in *The Steps to Freedom in Christ*. The process is intended to help you resolve any conflicts between you and your Heavenly Father through repentance and faith in Him. Essentially the process enables you to submit to God and resist the devil (James 4:7). Doing so eliminates the evil one's influence and connects you with God in a personal and powerful way. Now by the grace of God, you will be able to process the remaining steps for overcoming depression.

Second: Commit your body to God as a living sacrifice (Romans 12:1). After you have consulted the Great Physician, a visit to your doctor may be in order. Depression is a multifaceted problem that affects the body, soul, and spirit. Consequently, a comprehensive cure for depression will require a holistic answer. Many forms of biological depression can be diagnosed and treated. A disorder of the endocrine system can produce depressive symptoms. The endocrine system includes the thyroid, parathyroid, thymus, pancreas, and adrenal glands. The endocrine system produces hormones that are released directly into the blood system. The thyroid gland controls metabolism. An underactive thyroid (hypothyroidism) will cause mood changes, including depression. The metabolism of sugar is essential for maintaining physical and emotional stability. Hypoglycemia (low blood sugar) will likely be accompanied by emotional instability.

Women suffer from depression more than men due to their biological nature (or it may have something to do with who they are living with!). Archibald Hart said, "The reproductive organs of the female are extremely prone to creating mood swings. The depression at the onset of menstruation, premenstrual syndrome (PMS), the use of contraceptive pills, pregnancy, postpartum reactions, and menopause all revolve around the female's reproductive system. And as we currently understand it, the system is fraught with depression pitfalls."[10]

Many of the symptoms of biological depression can be eliminated when we assume our responsibility to live a balanced life of rest, exercise, and diet. To live a healthy life, we must be health-oriented, not illness-oriented. It is the same dynamic of winning the battle for your mind. The answer is not to renounce all the lies. The answer is to choose the truth. However, if you aren't aware that there are lies and if you ignore what your body is telling you, you will likely fall victim to disease and the father of lies. Whenever you start to sense that you are physically and mentally slipping back into a depression, don't just succumb to it; take charge of your life by praying as follows:

Dear Heavenly Father, I submit myself to You as your child, and I declare myself to be totally dependent upon You. I yield my body to You as a living sacrifice, and I ask You to fill me with Your Holy Spirit. I renounce the evil one's lies, and I choose to believe the truth as revealed in Your Word. I resist the devil and command all evil spirits to leave my presence. I now commit myself to You and my body to You as an instrument of righteousness. In Jesus' precious name, I pray. Amen.

Third: Be transformed by the renewing of your mind (Romans 12:2). Depression can be divided into two categories. One is related to lifestyle; the other is caused by a crisis event. Lifestyle depression can be traced to early childhood development or living in an oppressive situation that created or communicated a sense of hopelessness and helplessness. Our minds have been programmed over time to think negatively about ourselves, our circumstances, and the future. These negative thoughts and lies are often deeply ingrained. There have been thousands of mental rehearsals that have added to the feelings you are experiencing right now. The natural tendency is to ruminate on these negative thoughts. Daniel Goleman said, "One of the main determinants of whether a depressed mood will persist or lift is the degree to which people ruminate. Worrying about what's depressing us, it seems, makes the depression all the more intense and prolonged."[11]

Changing false beliefs and attitudes is necessary to overcome depression. The world will put you down, and the devil will accuse you, but you don't have to believe either one. You must take every thought captive to the obedience of Christ. In other words, you must believe the truth as revealed in God's Word. You don't overcome the father of lies by research or reason; you overcome deceiving spirits by revelation. God is not going to remove us from this fallen world's negativity. We are sanctified and protected by the truth of God's Word. Jesus said, "I have told you these things, so that in me you may have peace. In this world you will have trouble. But take heart! I have overcome the world" (John 16:33). Renewing our minds with truth takes active, sustained work. Every mental stronghold that is torn down in Christ makes the next one easier. Every thought you take captive makes the next one more likely to surrender. Lifestyle depression results from repeated blows that come from living in a fallen world. Rehearsing the truth, again and again, is the key to renewing your mind.

> " WE DON'T FEEL OUR WAY INTO GOOD BEHAVIOR; WE BEHAVE OUR WAY INTO GOOD FEELINGS. "

Fourth: Commit yourself to good behavior.

We are not instantly delivered from lifestyle depression. We have to grow out of it. It takes time to renew our minds, but it doesn't take time to change our behavior, which facilitates the process of renewing our minds and positively affects how we feel. We don't feel our way into good behavior; we behave our way into good feelings. If you wait until you feel like doing what is right, you will likely never do it. Jesus said, "Now that you know these things, you will be blessed if you do them" (John 13:17).

That is why some interventions for depression focus on behavior. Depressed people are helped when they schedule appointments and activities that pull them out of their negative mood. Go to work even though you may not feel like getting out of bed. Plan an activity and stick to it. Get more physical exercise and commit yourself to follow through on your plans. You may feel tired, but your body needs exercise. Start with a low-impact aerobics program or take walks with friends and family members. Continue routine duties even though you feel like you don't have the energy. These behavioral interventions or activities are only a start in developing a healthy lifestyle. If these are too difficult or physically impossible, then seek the kind of physical therapy that will get you back on your feet.

Stop living to eat and start eating properly to live. Balance your diet with 60% good carbohydrates, 30% proteins, and 10% healthy fats. Try to avoid processed sugars and high fructose corn syrup. Take a multivitamin and be sure that it includes D and B complex vitamins, especially B-12. B-complex vitamins help the adrenal glands deal with stress, and they are water-soluble, so they don't store in your system.

Certain negative behaviors will only contribute to depression. Drowning out your sorrows with drugs and alcohol is at the top of this destructive list. Although this may bring temporary relief, it will only further contribute to the depression.

Fifth: Seek meaningful relationships.

One of the major symptoms of depression is withdrawal from meaningful relationships. Isolating ourselves and being alone with our negative thoughts will only contribute to the downward spiral. You may feel like you want to be alone, but you need to stay connected to God and in contact with the right people. We absolutely need God, and we need each other. Wrong associations and relationships, however, will only pull you down. "Do not be misled: 'Bad company corrupts good character'" (1 Corinthians 15:33).

A frog was frolicking with his friends when another frog rubbed him the wrong way. Straying off from the pack, he hopped into a rut in the road. Two days later, he was still stuck in a rut. Some old friends came bouncing by and encouraged him to hop out of the rut, but he remained in the rut. Two days later, the friends saw him hopping around the pasture, and they asked what brought about the change. The frog said, "A Mack Truck came along, and I had to get out of there!" Sometimes we need someone or something to shake us out of our lethargy.

Sixth: Overcome your losses.

A loss can be real, threatened, or imagined. Any one of them can precipitate depression. How we respond to any loss or crisis will determine how fast we recover. The following steps will help you overcome your losses:

1. IDENTIFY EACH LOSS.

Concrete losses are easier to recognize than abstract losses. Changing jobs and moving to a new location can precipitate a depression even though it could improve your social status and financial base. The move may mean the loss of friends, community, and church. It will take some time to build new friendships and become part of a new church family. Many losses are multifaceted. For instance, the concrete loss of a job and wages may be accompanied by the abstract losses of self-respect, sense of worth, and collegial relationships. People don't react the same to losses because people have different values and different levels of maturity. To get beyond denial and into the grieving process, you must understand what you are losing or have already lost.

2. SEPARATE CONCRETE FROM ABSTRACT LOSSES.

Concrete losses are tangible, while abstract losses relate more to personal goals, dreams, and ideas. Abstract losses relate deeply to who we are and why we are here. Many concrete losses, such as losing a job, are contaminated with abstract losses. You may find a new job next week but remain depressed because you feel the pain of rejection and wrongly believe you are a failure. That is another reason why it is so important to understand who we are in Christ and find our acceptance, security, and significance in Him.

Separate real, imagined, and threatened losses. You cannot process an imagined or threatened loss in the same way you can a real one. In an actual loss, you can face the truth, grieve the loss, and make the necessary changes that make it possible to go on living in a meaningful way. A lawyer heard a rumor that his firm was going to be sued for services he performed. He thought, "I'm ruined. The firm is going down, and it is all my fault." Such thinking led to major depression and anti-depressant medications. I saw him a year later, and the company hadn't been sued. It was just imagined, but the depression was real.

3. CONVERT IMAGINED AND THREATENED LOSSES TO REAL LOSSES.

Imagined losses are distortions of reality. They are based on suspicions or lies that we have believed or assumptions that we have made. The mind doesn't like vacuums and will make assumptions when we don't know the facts. Seldom does the mind assume the best. We don't always act upon our assumptions, but if we do, we shall be counted among the fools because "where there is strife, there is pride" (Proverbs 13:10). People ruminate on various possibilities and consequences in their minds until they are depressed. The answer is to verify these assumptions and then follow Peter's advice, "Cast all your anxiety on him because he cares for you. Be alert and of sober mind. Your enemy, the devil, prowls around like a roaring lion looking for someone to devour. Resist him, standing firm in your faith" (1 Peter 5:7,8).

Threatened losses have the potential for being actual losses. These include the possibility of a layoff at work or a spouse who threatens to leave. Such threats can precipitate depression. It can be helpful to consider what the worst-case scenario might be and then ask yourself the question, "Can I live with it?" The answer is always, "Yes." By doing that, you are essentially processing the threat in your mind as an actual loss. The threat no longer has any power over you, and in that way, you are not letting any person or event determine who you are or keep you from being the person God created you to be.

4. FACILITATE THE GRIEVING PROCESS.

The natural response to any crisis is first to deny that it is really happening, get angry that it did happen, then try to alter the situation by bargaining with God or others. When that doesn't work, you feel depressed. You cannot bypass the grieving process, but you can shorten it by allowing yourself to feel the full force of the loss. The fact that certain losses are depressing is reality. It hurts to lose something that has value to you. You cannot fully process your loss until you feel its full force. That is probably what Jesus had in mind when He said, "Blessed are those who mourn: for they will be comforted" (Matthew 5:4).

5. FACE THE REALITY OF THE LOSS.

Only after you have faced its full impact are you ready to deal with the reality of the loss. This is the critical juncture. Are we going to resign from life, succumb to depression, and drop out, or are we going to accept what we cannot change and let go of the loss? We can feel sorry for ourselves for the rest of our lives, or we can decide to live with our losses and learn how to go on in a meaningful way. A prolonged depression signifies an over-attachment to people, places, and things that we had no right or ability to control.

6. DEVELOP A BIBLICAL PERSPECTIVE ON THE LOSS.

The trials and tribulations of life are intended to produce proven character. We suffer for the sake of righteousness. We can potentially come through any crisis as a better person than the one we were before. Losses are inevitable, and they are not intended to destroy us, but they will reveal who we are. People have discovered or deepened the awareness of who they are in Christ as a direct result of losses. Each subsequent loss only deepens that reality, perfects our character, and prepares us for an even greater ministry. We are all going to be victimized by losses and abuses. We can drown in our pity, blame others, claim that life isn't fair, and stay depressed for the rest of our lives. Or we can seek the Lord and develop a Biblical perspective about our loss. Whether we remain a victim is our choice. "For we who are alive are always being given over to death for Jesus' sake, so that his life may also be revealed in our mortal body" (2 Corinthians 4:11).

7. LET GO OF THE PAST.

A woman shared that her best friend ran off with her husband ten years earlier. This incredible betrayal deeply hurt her. She thought those adulterers had ruined her life, and there was nothing she could do about it. For ten years, she smoldered in bitterness and depression. Feelings of resentment and plots of revenge ruminate in her mind. Neil told her, "*I see you with one fist extended up to heaven where God has a firm grip on you. Your other fist is hanging on to your past, and you aren't about to let go. You are not even hanging on to God, but your heavenly Father is hanging on to you, His beloved child. Isn't it time to let it go? You are only hurting yourself.*" At the end of the conference, she worked through *The Steps*, and she let it go. The following day, she was singing in the church choir with the countenance of a liberated child of God.

She was a shining example of the following:

> Once I held in my tightly clenched fist... ashes. Ashes from a burn inflicted upon my ten-year-old body. Ashes I didn't ask for. The scar was forced on me. And for seventeen years, the fire smoldered. I kept my fist closed in secret, hating those ashes yet unwilling to release them. Not sure if I could. Not convinced it was worth it. Marring the things, I touched and leaving black marks everywhere...

> ...or so it seemed. I tried to undo it all, but the marks were always there to remind me that I couldn't. I really couldn't. But God could! His sweet Holy Spirit spoke to my heart one night in tearful desperation. He whispered, "I want to give you beauty for your ashes, the oil of joy for your mourning, and the garment of praise for your spirit of heaviness." I had never heard of such a trade as this: Beauty? Beauty for ashes? My sadly stained memory for the healing

in His Word. My soot-like dreams for His songs in the night? My helpless and hurting emotions for His ever-constant peace?

How could I be so stubborn as to refuse an offer such as this? So willingly, yet in slow motion and yes, while sobbing, I opened my bent fingers and let the ashes drop to the ground. In silence, I heard the wind blow them away. Away from me . . . forever. I am now able to place my open hands gently around the fist of another hurting soul and say with confidence, "Let them go. There really is beauty beyond your comprehension. Go ahead—trust Him. His beauty for your ashes.

Author Unknown.[12]

Overcoming Sexual Strongholds

Sexual sin runs deep in Christian culture and in our culture at large. The Centers for Disease Control and Prevention (CDC) reported that "on any given day in 2018, 1 in 5 people in the U.S. had a sexually transmitted infection (STI)," representing an all-time high. In 2018 alone, there were 26 million newly acquired STIs with nearly one in two of these acquired by people aged 15-24 years old. STIs are now considered a "national health threat."[1]

Porn statistics are even more sobering. Research by the Barna Group and Covenant Eyes reveals that initial exposure to porn begins in childhood and progresses. Men, women, teens, and young children are being caught up in the sexual trap of pornography and become enslaved. Many in the Church don't know how to address sex or sexual bondage, hoping the issue will simply go away, but with smartphones, social media, and the internet, sexual material is easily available at the click of a button. Those who attend church are not immune to it. Here are some of the conclusions by Barna Group and Covenant Eyes:[2]

- Over 40 million Americans are regular visitors to porn sites. The average visit lasts 6 minutes and 29 seconds.

- There are around 42 million porn websites, which total approximately 370 million pages of porn.

- The porn industry's annual revenue is more than the NFL, NBA, and MLB combined. It is also more than the combined revenues of ABC, CBS, and NBC.

- In the United States 47% of families reported that pornography is a problem in their homes. Pornography use increases the marital infidelity rate by more than 300%.

- Eleven is the average age that a child is first exposed to porn, and 94% of children will see porn by the age of 14.

- 56% of American divorces involve one party having an "obsessive interest" in pornographic websites.

- 70% of Christian youth pastors report that they have had at least one teen come to them for help in dealing with pornography in the past 12 months.

- 68% of church-going men and over 50% of pastors view porn regularly. Of young Christian adults 18-24 years old, 76% actively search for porn.

- 59% of pastors said that married men seek their help for porn use.

- 33% of women aged 25 and under search for porn at least once per month.

- 55% of married men and 25% of married women say they watch porn at least once a month.

- 13.57% of pastors say porn addiction is the most damaging issue in their congregation. 69% say porn has adversely impacted their church.

David Kyle Foster, the child of a Presbyterian pastor, gained some fame as a Hollywood actor. When he wasn't acting, he secretly lived a double life as a male prostitute. He longed for an emotional connection to his father, but he never seemed to get it. The lack of an emotional connection led him to believe his father did not love him, which led him down a dark path of sexual bondage looking to find love. His empty life finally drove him to Christ. He has become a powerful example of freedom and healing from sexual bondage and helps many others through his ministry, Mastering Life Ministries.[3] According to David's research[4], if you take any 16 people sitting in a row in any church, two will be struggling with their sexual orientation. Four will have been sexually abused. The "official" estimate is one out of every four women and one out of every seven men, but that is based only on what is reported. The more likely scenario is that one out of every three women and one out of every four men have been sexually abused. In the same row of sixteen people, an additional four will have unresolved sexual strongholds. That is true of every row in every church in America. We cannot ignore the sexual bondage that many are struggling to overcome.

Neil surveyed the student body of a conservative seminary and discovered that 60% of the male student body struggled with sexual guilt. Of that group, 50% said they would take an elective to help them overcome sexual strongholds if confidentiality was ensured. It wasn't offered! Imagine sending seminary graduates into the world who can't free themselves from their sexual struggles, much less help others. We can't be an effective disciple-making church without helping God's children overcome sexual strongholds, and we don't accomplish that by watering down God's standards.

YOU DIED TO SIN THE MOMENT YOU WERE BORN AGAIN.

Can we live a righteous life without sin? Can we choose not to sin? In Romans 6:1-13, Paul argues that we can because of our identity and position in Christ. It is important to note that the verbs in Romans 6:1-10 are past tense. There are no commands to obey. There are only statements to believe.

Paul begins by asking in verses 1-2, "What shall we say then? Shall we go on sinning so that grace may increase? By no means! We are those who have died to sin; how can we live in it any longer?" You may be wondering, "How do I die to sin?" You can't if you are a believer because you already died to sin the moment you were born again.

"We were therefore buried with him through baptism into death so that, just as Christ was raised from the dead through the glory of the Father, we too may live a new life. For if we have been united with him in a death like his, we will certainly also be united with him in a resurrection like his" (verses 4-5). If you identify with the death and burial of Christ, you must also identify with His resurrection and ascension. You have died with Christ, you have been raised with Him, and you are seated with Him in the heavens (Ephesians 2:6). From this position, you have all the authority and power you need to live the Christian life. Every child of God is spiritually alive "in Christ" and is identified with Him:[5]

- in His death (Romans 6:3,6; Galatians 2:20; Colossians 3:1-3)

- in His burial (Romans 6:4)

- in His resurrection (Romans 6:5, 8, 11)

- in His ascension (Ephesians 2:6)

- in His life (Romans 6:10-11)

- in His power (Ephesians 1:19-20)

- in His inheritance (Romans 8:16-17; Ephesians 1:11-12)

Paul continues, "For we know that our old self was crucified with him so that the body ruled by sin might be done away with, that we should no longer be slaves to sin" (Romans 6:6). Your old self was (past tense) crucified with Christ. The only proper response to this powerful truth is to believe it. You may be wondering, "What experience must I have for this to be true?" We don't make anything true by our experience. We choose to believe what God says is true and, by faith, choose to live in harmony with God. Then it works out in our experience. It is not what we do that determines who we are—it is who we are that determines what we do. We don't work in God's fields, hoping that He may someday love us. God already loves us, so we willingly and joyfully work in His fields.

> **IT IS NOT WHAT WE DO THAT DETERMINES WHO WE ARE—IT IS WHO WE ARE THAT DETERMINES WHAT WE DO.**

"Anyone who has died has been set free from sin" (Romans 6:7). Have you died with Christ? Then you have already been set free from sin. But I don't *feel* free from sin. If you only believe what you feel, you will never live a victorious life. You are not hypocritical if you live contrary to how you feel. That is what the devil wants you to believe. You are hypocritical if you are living contrary to what you profess to believe.

"Now if we died with Christ; we believe that we will also live with him. For we know that since Christ was raised from the dead, he cannot die again; death no longer has mastery over him" (Romans 6:8-9). Death has no mastery over us, but what about sin? Paul continues, "The death he died, he died to sin once for all; but the life he lives, he lives to God" (6:10). This was accomplished when "God made him who had no sin to be sin for us so that in him we might become the righteousness of God" (2 Corinthians 5:21). Since you are alive in Him, you are also dead to sin.

> WE DO NOT MAKE OURSELVES DEAD TO SIN BY COUNTING OURSELVES SO. WE COUNT OURSELVES DEAD TO SIN BECAUSE GOD SAYS IT IS ALREADY SO.

Many Christians believe that Christ died for the sins they have already committed but wonder about the sins they may commit in the future. When Christ died for all their sins, how many of their sins were still in the future? All of them! This is not a license to sin or to make grace increase, but a marvelous truth on which to live a righteous life and stand against Satan's accusations.

In verse eleven, Paul summarizes how we are to respond to what Christ has accomplished for us by His death and resurrection: "In the same way, count yourselves dead to sin but alive to God in Christ Jesus." We do not make ourselves dead to sin by counting ourselves so. We count ourselves dead to sin because God says it is already so. The verb "count" is present tense. In other words, we must continuously believe this truth and daily affirm that we are dead to sin and alive in Christ.

We don't have to sin, but we will since we have not fully experienced the completion of our salvation. We are saints who sin, but we do so less and less as we mature in Christ. John wrote, "My dear children, I write this to you so that you will not sin. But if anybody does sin, we have an advocate with the Father, Jesus Christ, the Righteous One" (1 John 2:1). We also have an adversary who accuses us day and night.

Death is the ending of a relationship, but not its existence. Sin is still powerful and appealing, and death is still imminent. But our relationship with both has changed because of our union with Christ. Paul explains how this is possible in Romans 8:1-2: "Therefore, there is now no condemnation for those who are in Christ Jesus because through Christ Jesus the law of the Spirit who gives life has set you free from the law of sin and death."

A law cannot be done away with, but it can be overcome by a greater law, which is "the law of the Spirit of life in Christ Jesus." To illustrate, we cannot fly in our own power because the law of gravity keeps us bound to earth, but we can fly in an airplane, which has the power to overcome the law of gravity. We cannot humanly stop sinning in our own strength, because the power of sin keeps us in bondage. But if we live by faith according to what God says is true, in the power of the Holy Spirit, we will not carry out the desires of the flesh. The importance of knowing who we are in Christ cannot be overstated.

DON'T PRESENT YOUR BODY TO SIN.

We believe what God has accomplished for us and that He will remain faithful, but we have a part to play as well. Paul continues, "Therefore do not let sin reign in your mortal body so that you obey its lusts" (Romans 6:12). According to this verse, our responsibility is not to allow sin to reign in our mortal bodies. How can we do that? Paul answers in verse 13 (NASB): "Do not go on presenting the members of your body to sin as instruments of unrighteousness but present yourselves to God as those alive from the dead, and your members as instruments of righteousness to God." Notice that there is only one negative action to avoid and two positive actions to practice.

Don't present the members of your body to sin.

We are not to use our eyes, hands, feet, or any part of our bodies in any way that would serve sin. When you see a sexually explicit program on TV and lustfully watch it, you are offering your body to sin. When you get inappropriately "touchy-feely" or flirtatious with a co-worker of the opposite sex, you are offering your body to sin. When you fantasize sexually about someone other than your spouse, you are offering your body to sin. Whenever you choose to offer parts of your body to sin, you invite sin to rule in your physical body.

Offer yourselves and members of your body to God.

Notice that Paul distinguishes between "yourselves" and "members of your body." Self is who we are on the inside - the immaterial or inner person renewed day by day (2 Corinthians 4:16). Dedicate yourself to God and commit your body to God as an instrument of righteousness. If you use your body as an instrument of unrighteousness, you will allow sin to reign in your mortal body. There is no way you could commit sexual sin without using your body as an instrument of unrighteousness, allowing sin to reign in your mortal body. That is why Paul wrote, "I urge you, therefore, brethren, by the mercies of God, to present your bodies a living and holy sacrifice, acceptable to God, which is your spiritual service of worship" (Romans 12:1 NASB). If you do that first, you will be more successful doing the next verse that instructs us to be transformed by renewing our minds. In 1 Corinthians 6:13-20, Paul has more instruction about the body, especially as it relates to sexual immorality:

> The body, however, is not meant for sexual immorality but for the Lord and the Lord for the body. By his power, God raised the Lord from the dead, and He will raise us also. Do you not know that your bodies are members of Christ himself? Shall I then take the members of Christ and unite them with a prostitute? Never! Do you not know that he who unites himself with a prostitute is one with her in body? For it is said, "The two will become one flesh." But whoever is united with the Lord is one with Him in spirit. Flee from sexual immorality. All other sins a person commits are outside the body, but whoever sins sexually sins against their own body. Do you not know that your bodies are a temple of the Holy Spirit, who is in you, whom you have received from God? You are not your own; you were bought at a price. Therefore, honor God with your bodies.

This passage teaches that we have more than a spiritual union with God. Our bodies are members of Christ Himself. Romans 8:11 declares, "And if the Spirit of him who raised Jesus from the dead is living in you, He who raised Christ from the dead will also give life to your mortal bodies through His Spirit, who lives in you." Our bodies are actually God's temple because His Spirit dwells in us. To use our bodies for sexual immorality is to defile the temple of God.

It is hard for us to fully understand the moral outrage felt in heaven when one of God's children uses His temple as an instrument of unrighteousness. It is even worse when someone defiles the temple of another person through rape or incest.

What happens when children of God—who are united with the Lord and one spirit with Him—also unite themselves to others through sexual immorality? The Bible says they become one flesh. They bond together. We can't fully explain it, but we have certainly seen the negative effect of such unions. Bonding is a positive thing in a wholesome relationship, but bonding only leads to bondage in an immoral union.

How many times have you heard of a Christian young woman who becomes involved with a man, has sex with him, and then continues in an unhealthy relationship? He mistreats her, and friends and relatives tell her, "He's no good for you. Get rid of him!" But she won't listen to them. Why? Because a spiritual and emotional bond has been formed. The two of them have become one flesh. Such bonds can only be broken in Christ.

In *The Steps to Freedom in Christ*, we invite inquirers to pray, asking the Lord to reveal to their mind every sexual use of their bodies as instruments of unrighteousness. God does, and He usually starts with their first experience, which may be incest or rape. Then for each one God brings to mind, they pray, "*I renounce the use of my body (having sex) with (the person's name), and I ask You to break that sexual bond spiritually, mentally, and emotionally.*" Then, they give their bodies to God as living sacrifices and pray that God would fill them with His Holy Spirit. Finally, they are encouraged to forgive those who have offended them. They forgive others for their own sake since nothing will keep them more bound to their past than unforgiveness.

In the cases of rape and incest, a person's temple is also defiled, even though they are the victim. "Not fair!" you say. Of course, it isn't fair—it is a violation of that person's temple. Although they have been victimized, they don't have to remain victims. They can renounce that use of their body and give it to God as a living sacrifice.

A local pastor asked us to help a young lady hearing voices. They were so real that she couldn't understand why we couldn't hear them. She had lived with a man who had abused her and sold drugs for a living. She was now living at home but was still attached to him. Near the beginning of the session, we asked her what she would do if we recommended that she never see him again. She said, "I would probably get up and leave." We suspected that would be the case, but we wanted the pastor to hear it. Encouraging her to make such a commitment is legitimate, but the timing is wrong.

After hearing her story, we asked if she would like to resolve the problems she was having in her life. She agreed, and we led her through *The Steps*. She renounced having sex with him and others, and she asked God to break the sexual, mental, emotional, and spiritual bonds. Then, she committed her body to God as a living sacrifice. There were no more demonic voices when we were done, and she seemed to be in complete peace. She had confessed her sin numerous times before without any sense of relief. Confession is the first step in repentance but doing that alone will not bring resolution. We shared with her how to maintain her freedom when she remarked, "I am never going to see that man again." That conviction came from God after she had removed the barriers to her intimacy with her heavenly Father. Before going through *The Steps*, she had no success winning the battle for her mind—a critical part of maintaining freedom in Christ- but now she could.

It may seem noble to say, "But if it were not for the grace of God I would stumble," but that implies that God's grace wasn't there for the person who stumbled, which is not true. It may also seem noble to say, "That will never happen to me," which a pastoral friend of ours said two weeks before he fell. "So, if you think you are standing firm, be careful that you don't fall! No temptation has overtaken you except what is common to mankind. And God is faithful; he will not let you be tempted beyond what you can bear. But when you are tempted, he will also provide a way out so that you can endure it" (1 Corinthians 10:12-13).

Jesus showed us the "way out" when Satan tempted him. After He had fasted for forty days and nights, the Holy Spirit led Him into the wilderness (Matthew 4:1-4). That is as vulnerable as anyone can be. He was on the verge of starvation and alone in the wilderness. Urging Jesus to turn the rock into bread was a real temptation when the human nature of Jesus was on the verge of starvation. Temptations appeal to legitimate, God-designed needs that we all have, but they steer us away from the One who can meet those needs according to His riches.

> **TEMPTATIONS APPEAL TO LEGITIMATE, GOD-DESIGNED NEEDS THAT WE ALL HAVE, BUT THEY STEER US AWAY FROM THE ONE WHO CAN MEET THOSE NEEDS ACCORDING TO HIS RICHES.**

The devil wanted Jesus to use His divine attributes independently of the Father in order to save His physical life. The same temptation came through the mouth of Peter that prompted Jesus to say, "Get behind me Satan! You are a stumbling block to me; you do not have in mind the concerns of God, but merely human concerns" (Matthew 16:23).

Jesus quoted Scripture in all three temptations, but what is often overlooked is that He said it aloud. Satan is under no obligation to obey our thoughts because he doesn't perfectly know them. Our protective armor includes "the sword of the Spirit, which is the word [*rhema*] of God" (Ephesians 6:17). In that passage, Paul used *rhema* instead of *logos*. *Logos* refers more to the content or character of the word. Whereas *rhema* implies the speaking out loud of God's Word. We should verbally resist the devil by saying something like, "Lord, I submit myself to You. Please fill me with your Holy Spirit. In the name of Jesus, and by His power and authority, I command Satan and all his demons to leave my presence." Those who struggle with addictive behavior are most vulnerable when alone in front of their computer. They won't feel embarrassed to confront the tempter out loud in such cases. When you are with others, mentally submit to God and ask for His divine presence to protect you.

When I was a young Christian, I (Neil) decided to clean up my mind. I had a relatively good upbringing, for which I am thankful, but I didn't become a Christian until my mid-twenties. After four years in the Navy, my mind was polluted with a lot of junk. I had seen enough pornography aboard a ship to plague me for years. Images would dance in my mind for months after one look. I hated it. I struggled every time I went to a store where pornography was being sold.

When I decided to clean up my mind, the battle got more challenging, of course. The temptation isn't much of a battle if you easily give in to it. It is fierce when you decide to stand firm in your faith. Think of your polluted mind as a pot filled with stale black coffee. It is dark and smelly. There is no way to get the polluting coffee out of the water because there is no delete button. However, sitting beside the coffee pot is a huge bowl of crystal-clear ice, representing God's Word.

Your goal is to purify the contents of the pot by adding ice cubes to it every day. I wish there were a way to dump all the cubes (words of the Bible) in at one time, but there isn't. Every cube dilutes the mixture, making it a little purer. You can only put in one or two cubes a day, so the process seems painfully slow at first. But over time, the water becomes less and less polluted, and the taste and smell of coffee decreases. The process continues to work provided you don't add more coffee grounds. If you read your Bible then look at pornography, the diluting process will not be as effective.

Paul writes, "Let the peace of Christ rule in your hearts, since as members of one body you were called to peace. And be thankful" (Colossians 3:15). The peace of Christ reigns in your heart when you "Let the message of Christ dwell among you richly" (vs. 16). The psalmist gives similar instruction: "How can a young person stay on the path of purity? By living according to your Word. I seek you with all my heart; do not let me stray from your commands. I have hidden your Word in my heart that I might not sin against you" (Psalm 119:9-11). Trying to stop thinking lustful thoughts won't work. Paul tells us what will work, "Whatever is true, whatever is noble, whatever is right, whatever is pure, whatever is lovely, whatever is admirable, if anything is excellent or praiseworthy, think about such things" (Philippians 4:8). We overcome the father of lies by choosing the truth!

You may find that winning the battle for your mind will initially seem like two steps forward and one step back. But gradually, it will become three steps forward, and one step back, then four and five steps forward as you learn to take every thought captive and make it obedient to Christ (2 Corinthians 10:5). You may despair with some steps backward, but God won't give up on you. Remember, your sins are already forgiven. This is a winnable battle because you are alive in Christ and dead to sin. The bigger war has already been won by Christ.

SEXUAL STRONGHOLDS

While Neil was speaking at a camp, a mother called and asked if she and her twelve-year-old son could spend an hour with him. The husband couldn't come, though he wanted to. This was a very close family of three. The young boy was a leader at school and church and gave the message one Sunday evening when the youth group was responsible for the service. The following Sunday morning, he was overwhelmed with homosexual thoughts toward the pastor. The boy had such a good relationship with his parents that he told them about it. That was highly unusual, and it was just as unusual that the parents knew what to do about it. They recognized where those thoughts were coming from. They instructed their son not to pay any attention to them and to keep choosing the truth, which he did. By the time they met with Neil, the tempting thoughts had all but subsided. Neil asked the boy, "Did you want to think those thoughts, and did you make a conscious choice to do so?" Of course, he didn't. The mother only wanted to know if there was anything else they needed to do.

Suppose a young boy is tempted by a sexual thought toward another boy at school. It is just a tempting thought, and it may have no impact at first. He knows nothing about taking every thought captive to the obedience of Christ or finding a way of escape. Suppose he dwells on those thoughts, even though he may believe it is wrong at first because he suspects it is abnormal. Thinking such thoughts will affect how he feels. That is the way God made us. So, he starts wondering, "If I am thinking these thoughts, then I must be gay!" That process may take months or even years to unfold, but he believes the lie one day, and he acts upon it with another boy or man. Now he has used his body as an instrument of unrighteousness, and he has allowed sin to reign in his mortal body. Most young people will keep that hidden for years, but one day they will likely step out of the closet and announce they are gay and walk away from their family and the Church.

As Neil has taught that information around the country, many have talked with him afterwards and shared that is precisely what happened to them. A university professor said, "I have feared for years that I was gay. I have a good marriage and family. I can't tell you what this insight means to me." Two years later, Neil was in the same area, and the professor came to help us minister to others. In those two years, he had helped over 60 men overcome their struggle with lust and homosexual tendencies.

In 1989, Marshal Kirk and Hunter Madsen published a book entitled; *After the Ball: How America Will Conquer Its Fear and Hatred of Gays in the '90s.*[6] They laid out a plan for normalizing behavior that had previously been viewed as deviant. **First,** desensitize the citizen to deviance by making deviancy appear positive. **Second,** make people feel guilty about their perceived bigotries, often equating homosexual and racial bigotry. **Third,** through the media, display as normal that had previously been viewed as abnormal. Liberal politicians in the United States have made the acceptance of homosexuality and same-sex marriage the next crusade for "civil rights." At the time of this writing, the homosexual community has more political clout in the United States than the evangelical community.

The liberal agenda in the homosexual community has highjacked 400 years of the African American experience of slavery, segregation and racism. Equating homosexuality with the struggle for racial equality has infuriated African American leaders who hold to the moral standards of the Bible. They have turned the hardship of the African American experience into a political agenda for their own selfish ambitions. Even though they are two separate issues, it has become increasingly difficult to stand against racism while at the same time maintaining a biblical standard for sexuality. If it does, the Church appears to be hateful and archaic to liberal progressivism.

God created us, male and female. So clear is that distinction that one's DNA sample can determine one's sexual identity. It was the soul that got damaged, and that can be repaired. God did not create anyone to be a homosexual, and our bodies are telling the truth. The Israelites were commanded under the Law to maintain that distinction. The moral standards of God have not changed. "Do not be deceived: Neither the sexually immoral nor idolators nor adulterers nor men who have sex with men nor thieves nor the greedy nor drunkards nor slanderers nor swindlers will inherit the kingdom of God" (1 Corinthians 6:9,10). Notice that sexual sins were the first four mentioned in this rogues' gallery.

We are called to make disciples and be ambassadors for Christ. Christ looked upon the multitude with compassion, and so must we. Those who refuse to believe and repent have a sure destiny of eternal separation from God, which should cause us to weep. Their sin has separated them from God, and we must be available to give an answer for the hope that lies within us. How they happen to manifest their sin is not the problem. It is just evidence that they are separated from God. They need the Lord, and it is our responsibility to offer them the gospel, which includes forgiveness and new life in Christ. After the apostle Paul corrected the ungodly behavior mentioned above (1 Corinthians 6:9,10), he wrote of authentic transformation, saying, "And that is what some of you were. But you were washed, you were sanctified, you were justified in the name of the Lord Jesus Christ and by the Spirit of our God" (verse 11). We have the opportunity to bring a message of hope, but it must be given with grace and compassion. We cannot teach the good news and be the bad news.

Tragically, the public perception of the conservative Church's stance on homosexuality has appeared more condemning than redemptive. In many cases, we have prohibited certain behaviors but not provided an adequate answer for those who wish to be rightly related to God. Condemning the behavior without giving them hope for overcoming sexual strongholds has caused many to reject the Church.

Suppose someone struggling with same-sex attraction attends your church, and they hear you correctly teach God's moral standard for sex. How do you think they would feel? Ashamed? Condemned? Not many are likely to come forward and admit their struggle. So they remain silent and hope no one will find out what they are struggling with. Couple that with the fact that a large majority of those who struggle with homosexual tendencies have been sexually abused. The last thing we want to do is add more abuse. We should have a lot more empathy for someone who is caught in this struggle than for heterosexuals who cheat on their spouses.

Although the Church has made serious errors in the past, we cannot compromise our commitment to the authority of God's Word. Such people can't be right with God if He said their behavior is an abomination to Him. If we genuinely care for another person's relationship with God, we have to help them remove the barriers to their intimacy with God through genuine repentance and faith.

God did not create people to be homosexuals or alcoholics. We can be genetically predisposed to particular strengths and weaknesses because of the fall. That alone doesn't make anyone a homosexual or an alcoholic. No attempt has been made to explain why others with a similar genetic predisposition aren't struggling with homosexuality or alcoholism. Furthermore, there is no demon of homosexuality zapping people with that affliction.

Such simplistic thinking has harmed the reputation of the Church. Clearly there is a spiritual battle for the mind that, when yielded to, can result in sexual immorality that could manifest as homosexual or heterosexual sin.

> **A DISCIPLE-MAKING CHURCH DOESN'T JUST PREACH ABOUT THE FREEDOM FOUND IN JESUS CHRIST; IT GIVES BELIEVERS THE TOOLS TO TRULY OVERCOME THE GUILT AND SHAME OF SEXUAL STRONGHOLDS AND WALK IN FREEDOM.**

In Romans 1:18-32, the apostle Paul explained our descent into sexual immorality. In summary, God has made Himself known in such a way that all are without excuse. To those who don't believe, God gave them up in the lusts of their hearts, to impurity, because they exchanged the truth about God for a lie. They worshiped and served the creature rather than the Creator. They still didn't repent, so God gave them up to dishonorable passions. They exchanged natural relations for those contrary to nature. Women burned in lust for other women, and men burned in lust for other men. They still didn't honor God, so He gave them up to a debased mind to do what ought not to be done. A reprobate or depraved mind is no longer capable of sound judgment. Such people are filled with all manner of unrighteousness, evil, covetousness, and malice. As a nation, we are clearly in moral decline and looking more and more like the decline of the Roman Empire, which took the same course.

Our ministry is to equip the Church to help those who desire to live a righteous life. This must begin with a spiritual check on our own biases. By that, we mean that we have to set aside our preconceived notions of how bad we think the sin is in order to love the inquirer. If we can't show the love of Christ, then we need to step aside and let someone else be the encourager. Love covers a multitude of sins.

Finding an intimate relationship with God will hopefully enable those coming out of a homosexual lifestyle to establish new healthy relationships with other believers. Such people are not gay Christians. The Bible never refers to believers by their flesh patterns or by who they were "In Adam." Being part of a loving and supportive community of believers is essential for complete recovery. It takes time to overcome a distorted self-perception and grow in the grace of God. Unfortunately, homosexuality has become the new leprosy for some conservative churches. We want to keep ourselves, our spouses, and our children away from such sinful behavior. This may be one of the biggest challenges we face. The goal is to become like Christ and not be like the Pharisees.

Patience is a virtue that must be cultivated when working with those who are struggling with addictive behaviors. Salvation pulls victims out of the swamp, but they are often covered with leeches, mud, and slime, which may cause some to shy away. Such attachments will slowly fall off as they mature. The Church must offer them acceptance and guidance because they may lose heart and return to the swamp. We can offer them Christ, but if we don't offer them a friend, we will likely lose them. This is true for every new believer. If we draw near to the throne of grace, we will receive mercy and find grace to help in our time of need (Hebrews 4:16). That is what we must offer those who desire to overcome addictive behaviors and live a righteous life.

"If you had the chance to overcome sexual strongholds and be free from the past without public embarrassment, would you take it?" Neil wrote on the back cover of *Winning the Battle Within*,[7] a book about overcoming sexual strongholds and addictions. We have no desire to expose anyone's sin, which is why Neil wrote the book the way he did. The questions at the end of each chapter discuss the truth and don't ask for personal disclosure, so the book can read in a group setting without anyone having to share intimate details if they don't want to. In the back of the book are *The Steps To Freedom in Christ*. We suggest that you finish the study by leading people through *The Steps*, allowing them to have their own encounter with God. If we don't offer them that opportunity, then very few people will come forward seeking help unless they are actually caught in the act of sin. A disciple-making church doesn't just preach about the freedom found in Jesus Christ; it gives believers the tools to truly overcome the guilt and shame of sexual strongholds and walk in freedom.

CHAPTER 10

Overcoming Addictions

When we were writing this book, the whole world was struggling with the coronavirus pandemic. At the same time, the United States was also struggling with racial tension and an opioid epidemic. While the former was not self-inflicted, the latter was. Growing up, Stephanie and I witnessed family members and friends in our neighborhoods abuse alcohol and drugs, most of which were self-inflicted. Weekends, Thanksgiving, Christmas, cookouts, or any other special occasions were good reasons to celebrate with drugs or alcohol. Whenever I saw people in my neighborhood drinking alcohol in excess, I remember thinking something didn't seem right, even though they made it seem like they were having a "good time." At the time, I did not understand that sometimes people use drinking or doing drugs to have a good time, relieve stress from a hard work week, or cope with the emotional pain they may be experiencing. Unfortunately for some, those "good times" turned into addiction and substance abuse problems that changed them into totally different people. Some people would become totally unrecognizable, often turning them from being nice and quiet to being angry at the world. Seeing people around us become slaves to alcohol and drugs was enough to turn Stephanie and I away from excessive drinking or using drugs. We were fortunate.

Results from the 2020 National Survey on Drug Use and Health provide some alarming statistics about the U.S. today. In 2020, among the 138.5 million people who drink alcohol, 61.6 million people (44%) are classified as binge drinkers and 17.7 million people (12%) as heavy drinkers. These numbers were highest among young adults aged 18 to 25. In addition, 25.9 million users of alcohol reported that they were using alcohol "a little more or much more" than they did before the COVID-19 pandemic began.[1] We'd like to think these stats are not true for people who faithfully attend church, but that's just not true. However, Christians are more likely to be secretive about their drinking than those who do not identify as Christians. In many evangelical churches, it isn't socially acceptable to drink excessively or gamble, so we opt for a more socially acceptable way of dealing with stress. We turn to food, our drug of choice, and call it fellowship. Casting our anxieties upon the refrigerator will not be healthy in the end (pardon the pun).

NON-BIBLICAL VS. BIBLICALLY-INFORMED GUIDANCE

Consider Nancy who is 50 years old and exhibits many maladaptive psychological, physical, and spiritual symptoms. She feels lethargic about life, struggles with interpersonal relationships at home, and doesn't seem to connect at church. She makes an appointment to see her doctor who discovers that her blood sugar levels are high, precipitated by her secret habit of drinking alcohol to excess. Although

Nancy is at least 75 pounds overweight, the doctor doesn't question her about her eating habits or lack of exercise. Her spiritual condition isn't even considered as an option for treatment, so the doctor gives Nancy a written prescription for an oral diabetes medication to treat her pre-diabetic symptoms.

Nancy dutifully takes her medication and makes an appointment to see her pastor. He listens patiently about her struggle with depression and family problems. He asks about her prayer and devotional life, which are virtually non-existent. He suggests that she spend more time with God daily and recommends a good book to partially replace her television "addiction." Meanwhile, she continues her eating habits and makes a halfhearted attempt to improve her spiritual disciplines.

The medication for her pre-diabetic condition gives her chronic indigestion, so she starts taking an H2 blocker like Tagamet which reduces her digestive symptoms. But now her stomach acid, which was low to begin with, is practically non-existent. Consequently, she's not digesting food, which reduces her nutritional input. The medication also puts more stress on her kidneys, and her estrogen level is low which results in a urinary tract infection.

Her doctor puts Nancy on antibiotics for the infection, but that lowers her immune system and kills most of the beneficial bacteria in her colon. The result is a bad case of the flu, which she can't seem to overcome, and she has constant gas from a colon imbalance. Nancy starts taking antihistamines for a sinus infection, and her doctor recommends a hysterectomy to solve her urinary tract infection. Nancy has the surgery and starts taking synthetic hormones, making her feel depressed and weepy. She sees a psychiatrist who prescribes an antidepressant. Nancy is now taking a diabetic medicine, an H2 blocker, antihistamines, synthetic hormones, an antidepressant, and a shot of gin when she needs it. She's exhausted all the time, mentally in a fog, emotionally withdrawn, and waiting for the next health problem to hit—which it will!

Let's start over again. Instead of seeing her doctor, Nancy decides to confide in a trained encourager at her church. After hearing her story, the encourager senses that Nancy has some unresolved personal and spiritual issues and invites her to attend a small group starting the *Freedom in Christ Course*. Nancy's inclination is to decline the offer because another night out sounds like too much work for someone so exhausted. The encourager reminds her that it would be good to get away from family responsibilities once a week and do something for herself for a change.

Reluctantly, she agrees to attend the class. The encourager recognizes that Nancy needs a lifestyle change and invites Nancy to come with her to the YMCA and start an exercise program that isn't too extreme. She meets a new friend at the Freedom in Christ class who shares how she lost several pounds by eating more healthily. They agree to meet and discuss proper nutrition.

Several months later, through her will and choices Nancy finds her freedom in Christ and discovers what it means to be a child of God and walk under the conviction and power of the Holy Spirit. With the encouragement of her friend, she has stuck it out at the YMCA, and her energy level has increased significantly, due partly to her new eating habits. She has lost twenty pounds, and her blood sugar level is normal. She has made some new friends at the Y and at the discipleship course group. This isn't rocket science. It is Biblically-informed common sense.

Many would agree that obesity is now the number one health problem in the United States, rising to the level of a "public health crisis." Today, nearly 40% of all adults over the age of 20 are obese, and it causes about 1 in 5 deaths in the U.S. a year.[2] Every year, we hear of a new revolutionary diet program, but people continue to put on the pounds. One common thread runs through every diet program and every secular recovery program. They are all law-based. There is either something you must abstain from or something you must do to follow them.

A newspaper featured an article by a woman commissioned by the state board of education to lecture students on safe sex. The assumption was, if students only knew the dangers of sexually transmitted diseases, they would behave properly. This woman had a major weight problem. Consequently, she had devoured books on nutrition, exercise, and diet. She probably knew enough to give lectures on those subjects as well, but knowing all that information did not stop her from having a second piece of pie before her first presentation. She realized from her own experience that telling people what they are doing is wrong does not give them the power to stop doing it. If that approach didn't work for her as an adult, how could she expect it to work for children?

For years the U.S. government ran the DARE program with the slogan, "Just say no!"[3] Did that work? No! Laying down the law doesn't work in the church either. Paul argued that the law could stimulate the desire to do what it had intended to prohibit (see Romans 7:5, 8). If you don't think that is true, try telling your children they can't play on the computer or get on their iPad until after dinner. The moment you say that, what do they want to do before dinner? God told Adam and Eve to eat from any tree in the garden, except for the tree of the knowledge of good and evil. Which tree was Eve tempted to eat from?

"He has made us competent as ministers of a new covenant, not of the letter but of the Spirit; for the letter kills, but the Spirit gives life" (2 Corinthians 3:6).

Many are unaware that a popular Twelve Step program was originally only six steps. Began by the Oxford Group, it was a Christ-centered Presbyterian program that showed good results. Others took note and wanted to use the program but didn't want to include God. Six more steps were added, a "higher power replaced the concept of God," and it ceased being a Christian ministry.[4]

> **REINFORCING A FAILURE IDENTITY IS COUNTERPRODUCTIVE TO BECOMING COMPLETE IN CHRIST. IN FACT, PAUL NEVER IDENTIFIES A BELIEVER BY THEIR FLESH PATTERNS.**

The turbulent sixties exposed many Christians needing help to overcome addictive behaviors, and the Church responded. Just as people tried to "Christianize" secular psychology, they attempted to "Christianize" secular recovery programs. With the programs came many beliefs that aren't consistent with Scripture and common sense instead. Let me name a few.

First, they instruct participants to "work the program because the program works." There is no program that can set anyone free. That is a law-based concept. The original six steps worked because of Christ, not because of the program.

Second, they teach that alcoholism is a disease and incurable. Once you are an alcoholic, you will always be an alcoholic. That is bad theology that sounds like "once a sinner, always a sinner." That is not true either. Once we were sinners, but now we are saints who occasionally sin. You can't expect to live a righteous life if your core identity is still sin. Calling addiction a disease supposedly makes them feel better, but it may also absolve some from assuming their responsibility to live righteous lives. "*It's not my fault. I have this disease!*" Sin is not a disease. Sin is what separated us from God when we were "sinners," and sin is what keeps us from an intimate relationship with Him when we become His children.

Third, recovery program participants introduce themselves as addicts, alcoholics, co-addicts, and co-alcoholics. Should not the Christian say, "Hi, I'm Daryl, I'm a child of God who is struggling with a certain flesh pattern, but I am learning how to overcome my addiction by the grace of God." Reinforcing a failure identity is counterproductive to becoming complete in Christ. In fact, Paul never identifies a believer by their flesh patterns. "So, from now on, we regard no one from a worldly point of view" (2 Corinthians 5:16).

Fourth, in these programs, the goal is sobriety. If abstinence is the goal, then Ephesians 5:18 would read, "Do not get drunk on wine… Instead, stop drinking." The Apostle Paul has a different answer, "Instead, be filled with the Spirit." And Galatians 5:16 says, "So I say, walk by the Spirit, and you will not gratify the desires of the flesh." What happens if you take alcohol away from someone addicted to it? You have a dry drunk, and the person will likely be more miserable than they were before. Plus, you took away their means of coping without giving them a better way. That is why 85% of individuals will return to their drug of choice within the year following treatment. In fact, many will relapse within weeks to months of just beginning any kind of addiction treatment.[5] Have you ever tried to take an old bone away from a dog? You will have a dog fight. Try throwing them a steak, and they will be a lot more willing to spit out the old bone.

Fifth, most recovery programs talk about dual diagnoses, but the reality is multiple diagnoses. Show us anyone who is addicted to anything, and we will show you someone who has a poor sense of worth, who is depressed, anxious, fearful, ashamed, angry, and bitter. Do you think they can resolve all of that plus their relational problems at home by abstaining? Additionally, the vast majority of people seeking treatment for chemical addiction are also sexually addicted, and, in most cases, that is not even addressed. They know that sexual addictions are more challenging to overcome than chemical addictions and much easier to cover up.

Finally, if you attend one of these self-help groups, you will hear phrases like, "You have to get rid of that stinking thinking," or "Don't pay attention to that 'committee' in your head." Most recovery programs do not take into account the reality of the spiritual world and don't acknowledge or understand the spiritual battle going on for their minds. Have you ever tried not to think of sexual thoughts or tempting thoughts? Did that work?

People abuse chemicals for three basic reasons. The first is peer pressure induced "party time." To have a good time, they have to get rid of their inhibitions. Everybody is doing it, and you don't want to be the party pooper! The nerd! The odd person out! The first puff on a cigarette, the first taste of beer, and the first sip of hard liquor are seldom, if ever, a good experience. So why do so many people proceed with an act that their natural senses reject? Very few young people are secure enough in their faith to stand alone when everyone else at school, work, or play is drinking and using drugs. They have a better chance if they have a Christian support group that accepts them for who they are and provides them a sense of belonging.

Second, some turn to chemicals to escape the pressures of life. This is what happy hour is all about. *I'll just stop off after work, have a couple of drinks, and maybe one for the road.* Our emotional development is arrested the moment we turn to chemicals to reduce our stress and cope with the pressures of living. Drinking to deal with stress or the anxiety of a troubled mind is the secular form for managing the soul. Masking anxiety with alcohol or any form of drugs can lead to a false sense of reality and lead to disaster.

Neil's attempt to help a couple was leading nowhere. The husband was struggling at work, home, and church. The husband thought everyone was wrong except him. Neil didn't see either of them for months. Then out of the blue, Neil got a call from the husband one evening. The man had just been released from jail after three months, and Neil was the first one he called. He said, "This is the first time that I have been clean in ten years." Neil had no idea that he had been abusing drugs, and his wife probably didn't know either. He had been selling just enough drugs at work to feed his addiction. Neil asked him, "Knowing that you were on the verge of losing your job, your wife, and even your church, why did you continue to use it?" He said, "That was the only time that I ever felt good about myself." Neil never forgot that statement because of what it did for him. Neil went from wanting to strangle the man to wishing he were present so he could hug him. How much more could we help such individuals if we understood their struggle and resultant self-loathing?

Third, people turn to medications to stop the pain. That is the major reason why people abuse prescription medications. If you have a banging toothache, you don't care about politics, other people, or world evangelization. You only want to stop the pain.

THE ADDICTION CYCLE

Euphoria
(Mellowed Out)

Rush
(Onset of
Reaction)

Addiction:
1. Habituation
2. Dependency
3. Tolerance
4. Withdrawal

Baseline Experience

Guilt
Fear
Shame

Grandiose, Aggressive
Behavior

Efforts to Control Fail
Repeatedly

Tries Geographical Escapes

Family and Friends
Avoided

Loss of Ordinary
Willpower

Tremors and Early Morning
Drinks

Decrease in Ability to Stop
Drinking

Onset of Lengthy
Intoxication

Moral Deterioration

Impaired Thinking

Drinking with Inferiors

Unable to Initiate Actions

Obsession with Drinking

All Alibis Exhausted

Occasional Drinking

Increase in Tolerance

Memory Blackouts

Excuses Increase

Surreptitious Drinking

Increased Dependency

Persistent Remorse

Promises Fail

Loss of Interest

Work, Money Troubles

Resentments
Pile Up

Neglect of Food

Physical
Deterioration

Irrational Fears

Obsessions

Physical Illness

Complete Defeat

Death or
Recovery

THE CYCLE OF ADDICTION[6]

There are many paths to addiction, but the cycle that spirals downward is similar for all those caught in the web of dependency. The chart on page 200 outlines the addiction cycle for alcoholics.[7] The "baseline experience" refers to people's mental and emotional state when they first begin to use drugs, drink, or gamble or encounter their first sexual stimulation. The first drink, puff, snort or sexual feeling brings an immediate reaction in their bodies, and they feel a rush. Alcohol and drugs don't step on the accelerator; they release the brake. There is a feeling of euphoria when the chemicals take effect, your date touches your leg, or the slot machine pays off with a pile of coins. Getting high can be fun for the moment.

The baseline experience is different for those looking for a reprieve from the pressures of life. They could be a bundle of nerves or depressed about their circumstances. They are looking for a high to lift their spirits or something to calm their nerves. Melancholic people just want to drown their sorrows. Alcohol or drugs will help them mellow out. It works! Within a matter of minutes, they feel better. The same is true for those who want to stop the pain. They can't wait for that rush to take effect. Then they will feel better.

Unfortunately, the effect wears off. The morning after is a different story. They wake up feeling just a little bit lower than their baseline experience. Reality sets in. They have a headache, and they hardly recognize the person in the mirror. They have to go to work or school, and all the pressures and responsibilities of life come rushing back. There may be a twinge of guilt, shame, or fear depending upon their conscience. For some, it could be a complete violation of everything they have ever been taught and believed. They vow they will never put themselves in a position of compromise again. For the party animal, it was very fun, and who doesn't want to have fun? They can hardly wait to do it again. They live from weekend to weekend, from party to party. They live for the euphoria. They get a rush just thinking about it.

The first step toward addiction is creating the habit. This pattern of behavior becomes the means to have a good time or to cope with life. A habit is a knee-jerk response—a flesh pattern. You feel pain, so you reach for the pills. You feel down, so you do something that will pick you up. You feel stressed out, so you reach for something that will calm your nerves. It worked before, so it will work again. You have trained yourself to depend upon something to pick you up, to stop the pain, to soothe your nerves, to make you feel good. You don't believe that you can have a good time or feel good without it. Occasional drinking, gambling, sexual activity, or using drugs has become a habit, a means of emotional support, a crutch to lean on.

When the effects wear off, the guilt, fear, and shame become more and more pronounced. With each successive use alcoholics and addicts get further and further away from their original baseline experience. They feel like the king of the hill when they are high. They are filled with grandiose ideas, and many become more aggressive in their behavior. They feel emboldened.

The downside is they begin to experience memory blackouts, and efforts to regain control of their lives fail repeatedly. *How did I get home last night? What happened? I better get a grip on myself; I'm starting to lose control!* Most alcoholics feel guilty about their behavior, so they begin to drink secretively. They leave familiar surroundings to go where people don't know them. They can't live with the shame.

Initially, all they want to do is reach that elusive high and euphoria they felt and experienced before. The problem? It takes more and more alcohol and a greater fix to achieve that original high. Every user develops a tolerance for their drug of choice. It may have taken two beers when they first started, and now it takes a case. Beer is too slow anyway; you need a chaser to speed up the process. Marijuana was fine at first, and now it takes cocaine. Aspirin used to stop my headache, and now it barely has an impact. The first kiss was exciting, leading to petting, but now you need to go further to experience that initial rush. The alcoholic and addict will never experience the euphoria they once did, no matter how much they drink or take. As the lows get lower, the highs get lower too. Before long, all they hope for is to get back to their baseline experience, but even that begins to elude them. They are the prodigal son who would rather go back home and be a hired man for their father, not realizing their father would welcome them as his child (Luke 15:17-23).

Their loss of willpower robs them of their ability to live a responsible life at home and work. The cost to support their habit almost always causes financial problems. Many white-collar workers may be able to support their habit for years and carry on their masquerade in public, but their families will suffer tremendous hardship. The poor will steal to support their addiction. The morality of both will deteriorate. They have no sense of worth nor any self-respect. They are disgusted with themselves. They don't eat well, and they don't care for themselves. Consequently, their physical health becomes a factor.

Those who have a reputation to uphold and suffer from a chemical addiction will start to withdraw from social contacts. They don't want their weaknesses to be seen or known, and they fear being publicly humiliated or exposed. They become paranoid about people looking at them or talking about them. They have no mental peace. Condemning voices haunt them day and night. *You're disgusting. Why don't you just check out? You're good for nothing. Your family would be better off without you.* The only way they know how to silence those voices is to keep feeding their addiction.

INTERVENTION

I don't have a drinking problem. I can stop at any time. The only way you can prove that to yourself and others is to stop. Unfortunately, many have to lose their job, family, and health before they will admit to their addiction. The same pride that keeps unbelievers from realizing their need for a savior keeps driven Christians from admitting they are acting as their own god. Brokenness is the key to any recovery ministry. If we don't take the initiative ourselves, God will orchestrate the process. That's what He did to save us! "Humble yourselves, therefore, under God's mighty hand, that he may lift you up in due time" (1 Peter 5:6).

> **THE SAME PRIDE THAT KEEPS UNBELIEVERS FROM REALIZING THEIR NEED FOR A SAVIOR KEEPS DRIVEN CHRISTIANS FROM ADMITTING THEY ARE ACTING AS THEIR OWN GOD.**

When we see others on a downward spiral, we can take the initiative and schedule an intervention. The intervention will be more effective if experienced, unbiased help is solicited outside the immediate family. Family members have often been too judgmental, condemning, or too busy covering up and pretending that all is well. An intervention gathers all the principal people (including the boss at work if applicable) in the alcoholic's or addict's life in a well-orchestrated time of confrontation. Some will rehearse the intervention without the alcoholic's knowledge. It should be scheduled at a time when he or she is sober. Each person then relates what the alcoholic's addiction is doing to them personally. The alcoholic or addict is given an opportunity to seek treatment, which has already been scheduled. Speaking the truth in love and holding your ground are the two most vital ingredients to get this person to seek the help they need.

CO-DEPENDENT NO MORE

The downward spiral that all addicts find themselves in is like a tornado that gathers up victims in its path and hurls them out of the way. The primary victims are family members. The spouse is the first affected. A faithful attendee and worker in our church made an appointment to see us. We hardly knew her husband since he was seldom seen with her at church. His wife had often requested prayer for his salvation, but she never shared the family secret. Twenty years of silence were broken that afternoon. She couldn't live that way any longer. His alcoholism had destroyed their family and their marriage.

For twenty years, she had been the classic enabler. If he couldn't make it to work because of his drinking, she covered for him. If he passed out drunk on the front lawn, she would somehow get him into the house, clean him up, and put him to bed. The children were told to do the same. They had to protect the family name and make sure the chief breadwinner didn't lose his job. Lying and covering up became the means of survival. Family members were threatened if they didn't play along, and even if they did play the game, they still suffered mentally, emotionally, and physically. The shame they bore kept them locked in silence. Enablers have learned to cope and survive by lying and covering up. The fear of retaliation keeps them silent. Their identity and sense of worth are shattered by what is happening at home. They believe they will lose their last shred of dignity by blowing the whistle. Some people would blame them for breaking up the family, which unfortunately happens in many abuse cases. The Biblical mandates to "speak the truth in love" (Ephesians 4:15) and "walk in the light" (1 John 1:7) are abandoned for self-preservation, but just the opposite is happening: self-destruction. They are in bondage to their lies and bitterness.

If someone is traveling down a road to destruction, do you want to enable the process? You will never help the addict or the abuser by enabling them to continue their irresponsible and immoral behavior. It will only get worse for both of you and undermine your relationship with God.

Turn them into their boss, their church, or even the police if necessary. We're not saying that because we don't care for them, but because we do care for them. They are like misbehaving little children that are screaming for attention, *"Doesn't anybody care enough about me to stop me from destroying myself?"* Discipline is proof of our love, not a violation of it. The fear of being exposed is worse than the actual consequences of getting exposed. They are tired of living a lie, and many are relieved when they are finally caught. The consequences of not doing anything are worse than the consequences of taking a stand, not just for the addict but for everyone involved.

WHERE DO WE START?

Many years ago, Neil was invited to speak at the Rescue Mission in Los Angeles to the men who had made a decision for Christ and were enrolled in their discipleship program. When he walked in, they all stood and applauded. He thought Billy Graham, or some other prominent person, had followed him in. Actually, they weren't applauding Neil. They were acknowledging what he stood for. They had been watching the DVD of the Freedom in Christ course. They were applauding the message he was going to share that morning which they had already heard on the DVD. *"Gentlemen, I want you to know that you are not a derelict, a bum, a drunk, an alcoholic, or an addict. You are children of God, and no, you have not committed the unpardonable sin."* The place erupted.

Most churches are not large enough to have a fully functioning recovery ministry, but that does not keep them from being a disciple-making church. Every church can offer an opportunity to repent and find identity and freedom in Christ. If that is successful, then almost any program will work. However, a well-thought-out, Biblically-based program staffed by trained encouragers will bear more fruit than a poorly thought-out program staffed by novices. Unfortunately, dedicated incompetency is still incompetency.

When Neil taught at Talbot School of Theology, he required the students to attend an Alcoholics Anonymous meeting (AA) and report their experience.[8] Most wrote that they struggled with the smoke and the foul language, but almost everyone said, "I wish I could get my class or small group at church to be that honest." Most AA participants have already had their sins exposed, so there is nothing to cover up. We have no problem recommending the services of AA. Their twelve steps can be understood from a Christian perspective, and they know a lot about addiction. They have saved many natural lives and provided the necessary support to start again. It is not what Christian AA groups offer that we struggle with; it is what they are not offering, which is a liberated life in Christ. Your church can offer that.

CHAPTER 11

Overcoming Marriage
Brokenness

From the turbulent 1960s to 2010, the Christian community made a massive effort to save the family. Focus on the Family was the largest Christian radio ministry ever. Degree programs on marriage and family ministries were offered in almost every Christian university and seminary. There was an endless number of books and videos specifically addressing marriage and family issues. Saving marriages and families may have been the greatest felt need in the Christian community.

Today, with all of these resources available, how are we doing? Has the family as a whole become stronger in the United States and around the world? Have our marriages become better? In the last couple of decades, the number of U.S. children living with a single parent has risen as marriage rates have declined. According to a Pew Research Center study, the United States has the world's highest rate of children living in single-parent households—almost a quarter (23%)![1] Children raised by both of their biological parents are in the minority. Over eighty percent of African American children are born out of wedlock.[2]

Homosexual marriages are more and more common, and the gay community has more political clout than the evangelical community due to rampant moral failure among Christian leaders.

A respected doctor shared that he and his wife were having marriage problems. He arranged for them to attend a weekend marriage retreat taught by a well-known Christian author. He said, "The content was excellent, but we argued all the way there and back." What is missing?

> **IT ISN'T INTENTIONAL, BUT BIBLICAL INSTRUCTION CAN BE A SUBTLE FORM OF CHRISTIAN BEHAVIORISM, I.E., TRYING TO CHANGE BEHAVIOR WITHOUT CHANGING THE PERSON.**

It isn't intentional, but Biblical instruction can be a subtle form of Christian behaviorism, i.e., trying to change behavior without changing the person. "You shouldn't do that. You should do this, or here is a better way to do it." That may not be legalism in a Pharisaic sense, but, in some cases, the emphasis has shifted from "negative" legalism (don't do this and don't do that) to "positive" legalism (do this and do this and do this and do this, ad nauseam). There is nothing positive about legalism regardless of its emphasis. When applied to marriage, such counsel sounds like:

> Mr. Fitzgerald, have you loved your wife as Christ loved the Church? Would you be willing to do that if you knew how? Let me suggest some practical ways to do that, and possibly some behaviors and words that would be best left undone and unsaid. Mrs. Fitzgerald, have you respected your husband as the head of your home? My wife would be happy to share with you what she has learned after years

of living with me. Do you suppose you both could do that for each other? Good! I'm going to give you an exercise on marital communication that I would like for you to work through this week. Let's meet again next week at this same time and see how you are doing.

Pointing out our Biblical roles and responsibilities and suggesting how to accomplish them may be appropriate in the right circumstances. However, trying to get people to behave more appropriately as a couple when they are torn up on the inside will not work. That would be like trying to teach two people how to dance when one or both are on crutches. How can they become one in Christ if neither one is experiencing their freedom in Christ? What is missing is a liberated life in Christ.

A Christian marriage is a spiritual union with God, and it is intended to be a visible expression of the relationship that God has with the Church, which is the bride of Christ. Notice how they are intertwined in Ephesians 5:25-28:

> Husbands love your wives, just as Christ loved the church and gave himself up for her to make her holy, cleansing her by the washing with water through the word, and to present her to himself as a radiant church, without stain or wrinkle or any other blemish, but holy and blameless. In this same way, husbands ought to love their wives as their own bodies.

We cannot do in our own strength and resources what only God by His power can do through us. What makes this so subtle is that all the instructions in the example above could be Biblically sound but spiritually dead. It may not be that what we are doing is wrong. It is more a case of what is missing. It is like a new car trying to fulfill its purpose when it's out of gas. Of course, we want people to behave according to God's standards, but they never will if they are disconnected from God. To bear fruit, we must be connected to the source of life.

"This is my Father's glory, that you bear much fruit, showing yourselves to be my disciples" (John 15:8). It would be a mistake to put more pressure on ourselves and others to bear fruit. What we have to do is abide in Christ. Bearing fruit is the evidence that we are abiding in Christ. "I am the vine; you are the branches; the one who remains [abides] in me and I in him bears much fruit; for apart from me you can do nothing" (John 15:5 NASB). Without Christ, we are not just handicapped. We are not just limited in what we can do. Without Christ, we can do nothing of eternal significance! We are incomplete without Him, and our marriages are as well. To maintain a Christian marriage, we have to become one "in Christ." Just saying we are won't change anything. It must be individually appropriated through repentance and faith. Suppose you have a church full of people in the bondage of bitterness or other unresolved conflicts. In that case, you have a church full of hurting marriages misrepresenting God; essentially you have a hurting church. The whole cannot be greater than the sum of its parts.

There are scriptural passages that relate to marriage and family in the Old Testament and in the second half of Paul's epistles, which are generally divided into two sections. The first half of Paul's epistles is theological (indicative), and the second half is practical (imperative). Those who oversee marriage and family ministries focus their attention on the practical aspects of Christian living, which are located in the second half of Paul's epistles. We firmly believe that if we can help people appropriate the first half of Paul's epistles, which establishes them in Christ, they will be able to live out the second half supernaturally.

We can't expect men to behave like Christian husbands when they are plagued by guilt, shame, or anger. We can't expect women to behave like Christian wives when they don't know what it means to be a child of God. To fulfill these roles, they both need to know who they are in Christ. To put it bluntly: *Forget your marriage; you are so torn up on the inside that you probably couldn't get along with your dog right now! But if you are willing to be honest about your internal struggles and get radically right with God, then there is great hope for your marriage.*

A pastor asked Stephanie and I if we would counsel a young couple who were living together but not married. Like many young couples today, they were living together because it helped their financial picture. The young lady was married before and wanted this relationship to be better than her previous one, which was emotionally and physically abusive. This lovely young couple came in very hungry for truth. They both were Christians but were living according to their flesh (logic) and not according to the Spirit (Romans 8). They were like two travelers lost in the desert and thirsty with no water to drink. God had already prepared their hearts for hearing and receiving the truth of understanding their identity and who they were in Christ. They both were ready for a clean drink of water: "Whoever drinks of the water that I will give him shall never thirst; but the water that I will give him will become in him a fountain of water springing up to eternal life" (see John 4:14 NASB). They both were receptive, and with every meeting, you could see the chains broken from their lives. When the Lord led us, we asked them why they were living together and not married. The young lady knew it was wrong and wanted to make it right. It was as if she was waiting for us to ask the question so she could finally bring what was in the darkness out into the light.

We asked if they would be willing to sleep in separate rooms and stop sleeping together. It was tough on the young man, but they both agreed. We took them through *Victory Over the Darkness* for the next eight weeks. When we got to Chapter Eleven on "Healing Emotional Wounds from Your Past," we led them through the twelve steps of forgiveness. They both were set free from painful issues from their past. As they both worked through their forgiveness issues, my wife and I asked if they would like to be reconciled to God by getting married instead of waiting for their destination wedding. We offered a private ceremony right in our office. They were ready! It was no surprise that they agreed. My wife made the office look beautiful. Their parents came from out of state to take part in this special moment. The six of us had a wonderful time seeing God redeem the lives of two of his children. Today, they are flourishing in their relationship with each other and with the Lord. They have worked through the ten-week *Freedom in Christ Course* and are telling others about their story. They are now taking other couples through VOD as a small group study.

We have seen stories like this happen numerous times with couples who have gone through the *Freedom in Christ Course*. Marriage is hardly even mentioned, and yet we have seen previously troubled couples walk out hand in hand after discovering their own identity and freedom in Christ.

This happened to us when we first attended a Freedom in Christ conference. Hundreds of other people have shared with our FICM office that it saved their marriage. Many more have shared the same result in response to reading *Victory Over the Darkness* and *The Bondage Breaker*, which only allude to the subject of marriage.

It is possible to have a house full of Christians and not have a Christian home. If just one family member has a root of bitterness, the whole family can be defiled. The other family members sense the tension in the home and either work together to heal the wounds or drift apart. Have you ever noticed that when the spiritual tide is out, all the tadpoles want to swim in their own little tide pool? When the spiritual tide is in, they all swim harmoniously together as though somebody other than themselves is orchestrating every move. Having a Christian home must begin with marital reconciliation, and reconciliation starts with individuals resolving their personal and spiritual conflicts.

STEPS TO SETTING YOUR MARRIAGE FREE[3]

Being fully reconciled to God makes it possible to be reconciled with one another. Trying to unite fallen humanity on any other basis than Christ has always failed. We are to be merciful to others as God has been merciful to us. We forgive others as God has forgiven us. We love because we have first been loved. A ministry of reconciliation must always begin with God. If that is successful, then we are free to give others what God has freely given to us.

Under the same premise that makes the individual *Steps to Freedom in Christ* so effective—namely, the inclusion of God through prayer— Chuck Mylander and Neil developed *The Steps to Setting Your Marriage Free*. Essentially it is a corporate repentance process that is dependent upon the presence of God. He is the One who grants repentance. It begins with a prayer of commitment by both husband and wife. Then each step begins with the couple praying together, asking the Lord to guide them. Each spouse sits silently before the Lord and individually works on their own issues.

The one absolute rule is that each spouse must deal with their own issues and not deal with their spouse's issues. For some, that is a tough rule to follow. In other words, they cannot play the role of the Holy Spirit in the other person's life. The process breaks down if one person will not assume responsibility for their attitudes and actions. In such cases, we have a modified version of *The Steps to Setting Your Marriage Free* that the responsible husband or wife can process independently. Nobody is keeping the responsible spouse from being the husband or wife that God created them to be. Assuming their responsibility preserves their intimate relationship with God, and that is the best way to save the marriage in the future.

After each spouse has dealt with their own issues before God, they are invited to come back together and share with each other. Usually, that includes some confession and asking the other to forgive them. *The Steps* include:

> 1. LEAVING MOTHER AND FATHER: In what ways have either spouse not left their parents physically, spiritually, mentally, emotionally, or financially? Many well-intentioned, and not so well-intentioned, parents have ruined the marriages of their children. Some newlyweds are still dependent upon their parents instead of God and each other.

> 2. BREAKING CYCLES OF ABUSE: This step has two parts. First, because sins and iniquities are passed on from one generation to another, each spouse must assume

responsibility for what they bring from their heritage into the marriage. Blood runs thick, so it is best not to criticize your spouse's family, and we need to be honest about our own. Second, couples have sinned together, which is best resolved by mutual agreement and confession.

3. BALANCING RIGHTS AND RESPONSIBILITIES: In troubled marriages, spouses attack the character of each other while looking out for their own needs. We must be responsible for our character and seek to meet the needs of each other. In what ways haven't I loved, accepted, respected, submitted to, or appreciated my spouse? In what ways have I tried to control my spouse, and in what ways haven't I trusted God to bring conviction to my spouse so that he or she can be filled with the Spirit and have self-control?

4. BREAKING SEXUAL BONDAGE: We never have the right to violate our spouse's conscience, and we cannot use the body of another to satisfy our lust. Good sex does not make a good marriage, but a good marriage will have righteous and mutually satisfying sex.

5. RELEASING OLD HURTS: Forgiveness is the glue that holds a marriage together.

6. UNMASKING SATAN'S DECEPTIONS: Christian marriages are under siege, and couples must know how to recognize Satan's strategies and still stand firm in their faith.

7. RENEWING THE MARRIAGE: This is a powerful step of committing your marriage, home, and family to the Lord. The process concludes by the couple holding each other's

hands and repeating their marriage vows. However, instead of saying, "I take you to be . . . etc." We say, "I give myself to you to be your wedded husband (wife), etc."

We would never ask someone to do something that we weren't willing to do ourselves. After many years of marriage, there were some issues that we had swept under the carpet, but God has a loving way of pulling the rug out from under us. Thank you, Jesus! It is amazing how we can let minor issues fester by falsely believing that it would be better for the relationship to ignore them than seek resolution.

Some Christian leaders were invited to participate in a *Setting Your Marriage Free* weekend retreat. They were asked to give some feedback at the conclusion, and this is what they wrote:

> The ineffectiveness of most churches is due to the ineffectiveness of marriages. I have tried all kinds of counseling, but the process in *Setting Your Marriage Free* deals directly with the source of the conflict and brings a life-changing transformation. God used this process to resolve all known strongholds that bound us. We are experiencing purification and holiness in all areas of our marriage. Yes, it was difficult. Through honest and vulnerable discussion, the Lord led us through problems, anguish, hurts, and fears, all the way to forgiveness, resolution, love, and commitment. It opened my eyes to the spiritual forces that would destroy our marriage, and it gave us the tools to win. I have been to marriage seminars, attended your conference, and read books on marriage, but this broke the strongholds in our

marriage and allowed us to continue in ministry. This cuts through the "religion" of society and puts us back on Christ's team, in the Word, focused on Him, and entering His work. This was my last resort, and I was apprehensive. But this real, honest, heartfelt, truthful, godly way softened my heart, gave me back my hope and a desire to love my husband. The Lord got to the heart of our dysfunction. Most of our work on our marriage had been 90% psychological and 10% spiritual. This was 100% spiritual without ignoring the psychological. Freedom is found in Christ individually first—then as a couple. This method and material got us beyond the surface into the cancer and finally free. This process gets to the heart of the issues, provides a format for dealing with them, and brings the truth of God's Word coupled with God's strength to resolve them. This was a powerful and meaningful experience for us. The Lord performed significant work in our marriage. This gave us a clean slate. After 20 years, we wanted a fresh start, and we got it.

GROWING THROUGH COMMITTED RELATIONSHIPS

God's primary way of developing Christian character in our lives is through committed relationships. First, marriage is a covenant relationship and was intended to last until one spouse physically dies. It is not a contract to rip up if the other defaults. Homes are like pressure cookers. We either get well done, or we blow the top off. There will be trials and tribulations when we live together in the confinement of our homes. "Therefore, as God's chosen people, holy and dearly loved, clothe yourselves with compassion, kindness, humility, gentleness, and patience. Bear with each other and forgive one another if any of you has a grievance against someone. Forgive as the Lord forgave you. And over all these virtues put on love, which binds them all together in perfect unity" (Colossians 3:12-14). We should stay true to our commitments, honor our obligations, remain faithful to our vows, and grow up. Where better are we going to learn to love, accept, and forgive one another? If we don't learn it in marriage, where will we? We agree with the following: *Marriage License—A Learner's Permit.*[4]

- It's a wise groom who has to be dragged to the altar. He knows what love is. It's death! If the lovers don't know this, they are headed for trouble. Never will you have your way again. You can't be happy if the other person isn't. No matter who wins the argument, you lose. Always. The sooner you learn this, the better off you'll be.

- Love is an exercise in frustration. You leave the window up when you want it down. You watch someone else's favorite television program. You kiss when you have a headache. You turn the music down when you like it loud. You learn to be patient without sighing or sulking.

- Love is doing things for the other person. In marriage, two become one. But the one isn't you. It's the other person. You love this person more than you love yourself. This means that you love this person as he or she is. We should ask ourselves frankly what that impulse is that makes us want to redesign the other person. It isn't love. We want the other person to be normal, like us! But is that loving the other person or ourselves?

- Love brings out the best in people. They can be themselves without artificiality. People who know they're loved glow with beauty and charm. Let this person talk. Create the assurance that any idea, suggestion, the feeling can be expressed and respected. Allow the other person to star once in a while. A wife's joke doesn't have to be topped. Don't correct your husband in the middle of his story. Cultivate kind ways of speaking. It can be as simple as asking them instead of telling them what to do.

- Don't take yourself too seriously. Married life is full of crazy mirrors to see ourselves—how stubborn, how immature we really are. You may be waiting for your wife to finish because you never lifted a finger to help her. Love is funny. Its growth doesn't depend on what someone does for you. It's in proportion to what you do for him or her. The country is swarming with people who have never learned this. So are divorce courts.[5]

There is a second reason why God primarily works in our lives through committed relationships. We can put on a public face for our neighbors, co-workers, and casual friends, but we can't be phony at home. Our children and spouses will see right through us. When we keep something from our spouses, they may not know what is wrong, but they will definitely know something is wrong.

An executive for a Christian denomination once asked Neil out for lunch. He said, "I have heard you say that we can't be our wives' counselor or pastor, and I agree with that. In many ways, my wife has been a very good spouse and mother and serves God by being the administrator in the church we attend. However, my wife needs some help, and she is open to it, but I also know that I am not the one to give it to her. Would you be willing to meet with her?"

In their first meeting, she shared her story, which didn't include any major abuses or conflicts. She said that she was raised in a good Christian home and was introduced to God at a very early age. She had what she thought was a good marriage and two fine children. She was a well-groomed, articulate lady who exemplified Christian professionalism. There was nothing obvious in her story that would precipitate the personal struggles she was presently having. They agreed to meet the following week and go through *The Steps to Freedom in Christ*. After they finished the process, she paused at the door on the way out and said, "It wasn't a good family that I was raised in, was it?" For years she had perpetuated the lie that it was. A month later, Neil received the following letter:

> How can I say thanks? The Lord allowed me to spend time with you just when I was concluding that there was no hope for me to ever break free from the downward spiral of continual defeat, depression, and guilt.
>
> Having literally grown up in church and being a pastor's wife for 23 years, everyone thought I was as put together on the inside as I was on the outside. On the contrary, I knew that there was no infrastructure

on the inside, and, often, when the weight of trying to hold myself together would cause my life to fall apart and come crumbling down, it seemed as if sheer determination was the only thing that kept me going.

When I left your office last Thursday, it was a beautiful crystal-clear day with the snow visible on the mountains, and it felt like a film had been lifted from my eyes. The radio was playing an arrangement of "It is well with my soul." The words of the song fairly exploded in my mind with the realization that it was well in my soul for the first time in years.

The next day in the office, my immediate response to "How are you today?" was, "I'm doing great! How about you?" In the past, I would have mumbled something about being almost alive. The next comment I heard was, "Boy, something must have happened to you yesterday."

I have heard the same songs and read the same Bible verses as before, but it is as if I'm really hearing them for the first time. There is an underlying joy and peace in the midst of the same circumstances that used to bring defeat and discouragement. For the first time, I have wanted to read my Bible and pray. It is hard to contain myself—I want to shout from the rooftop what has taken place in my life.

Already the deceiver has tried to plant thoughts in my mind and tell me that this won't last; it is just another

gimmick that won't work. The difference is that now
I know those are lies from Satan and not the truth.
What a difference freedom in Christ makes!

How do you think that changed the dynamics of their marriage and the environment at work? From a broad perspective, Biblical history moves from creation and freedom to the fall; from the fall to redemption; from redemption to repentance and faith; and from repentance and faith to freedom. "It is for freedom that Christ has set us free" (Galatians 5:1), but you won't experience that freedom if you don't know or believe the truth and haven't repented. From a narrower perspective, Paul's message brings us from spiritual death to life in Christ followed by instructions to put off the old self (who we were in Adam) and put on the new self (who we are in Christ). Then Paul brings up the subjects of marriage, family, and slavery. Being a slave in those days was very different from modern-day slavery, which is forced submission. A slave was more like an employee, and their physical needs were better met by serving their masters than trying to make a living independently. It was usually a lifetime assignment and a committed relationship like marriage.

Knowing who we are is the foundation for how we live. The barriers that separated us because of our natural heritage no longer exist: "Here there is no Gentile or Jew, circumcised or uncircumcised, barbarian, Scythian, slave or free... but Christ is all and is in all" (Colossians 3:11). In other words, "in Christ" there are no racial, religious, cultural, or social distinctions. Galatians 3:28 adds... "nor is there male and female, for you are all one in Christ Jesus."

However, becoming a new creation in Christ does not eradicate social roles, sexual gender, or lines of authority. For instance, in Colossians 3:11, Paul says there is no slave, then he refers to slaves in Colossians

3:22. Verse 11 refers to the identity of every child of God, and Verse 22 refers to the social situation in which someone may be called to live. Saying there is neither male nor female did not change the roles of husband and wife, nor did it change our gender. Christian fathers, mothers, children, and employees should live like children of God. Their identity in Christ is the same, and they carry equal status in the kingdom of God; but their roles in society are different. Remember, it isn't what we do that determines who we are. It is who we are that determines what we do.

Contrary to popular belief, freedom is *not* found in the exercise of choice; it's not a license to do whatever the flesh desires. Instead, freedom is related to the consequences of the choices we make. People may believe they have the freedom to tell a lie, but they would have to remember who they told a lie to and what the lie was. They would also have to live with the consequences of telling a lie, leading to a loss of trust and severed relationships. Exercising your "freedom of choice" to lie to your spouse can never end well. Christians are free to become all that God intended them to be.

> " CONTRARY TO POPULAR BELIEF, FREEDOM IS NOT FOUND IN THE EXERCISE OF CHOICE; IT'S NOT A LICENSE TO DO WHATEVER THE FLESH DESIRES. INSTEAD, FREEDOM IS RELATED TO THE CONSEQUENCES OF THE CHOICES WE MAKE. "

They are free from the attachments of the world, the flesh, and the devil.

The world's definition of love (*eros* and *phileo*) is very different from God's love (*agape*).[6] Eros is erotic or sensual love, which is a self-satisfying pleasure. *Phileo* is brotherly love. Jesus said, "If you love those who love you, what credit is that to you? Even sinners love those who love them" (Luke 6:32). *Phileo* is conditional love. God's love is unconditional because it is not dependent upon the object of one's love. God loves us because God is love (1 John 4:8). It is His nature to love us. When *agape* is used as a noun, it refers to the character of God. "Love is patient, love is kind. It does not envy, it does not boast, it is not proud. It does not dishonor others, it is not self-seeking, it is not easily angered, it keeps no record of wrongs. Love does not delight in evil but rejoices with the truth. It always protects, always trusts, always hopes, always perseveres. Love never fails" (1 Corinthians 13:4-8). If we all loved like that, what kind of marriages would we have?

When freedom and love are disjoined from the character of God, they become license and selfishness. "The goal of this command is love, which comes from a pure heart and a good conscience and a sincere faith" (1 Timothy 1:5). "For you were called to freedom, brothers, and sisters; only do not turn your freedom into an opportunity for the flesh, but through love serve one another" (Galatians 5:13, NASB). We may not be able to change what the world does, but the world cannot keep us from having a loving relationship with our spouses. "For this is the will of God, your sanctification; that is, that you abstain from sexual immorality; that each of you know how to possess his own vessel in sanctification and honor, not in lustful passion, like the Gentiles who do not know God"[7] (1 Thessalonians 4:3, 4 NASB).

After we went through Neil's training, we were forever changed. Our marriage became healthy, and our love for each other deepened. Neil told us we had a story to tell that would help others find their freedom in Christ. We will be celebrating thirty years of marriage in April of 2022. We were invited to work full-time for other ministries, but God clearly led us to be on staff with Freedom in Christ Ministries. It was a difficult decision for us. The task of raising our support challenged our faith, but it improved our lives. Now, God has given us the wonderful opportunity to minister to college and professional coaches, professional athletes, churches, struggling married couples, single adults, and families. All have profited from discovering who they are in Christ as we have.

As children of God, we are no longer enslaved to sin. We are bondservants of Almighty God. We gave Him our lives, and He gave us His. That was the best exchange we have ever made. We pray that you, too, will find freedom in Christ from a life of slavery to sin.

ENDNOTES

ENDORSEMENTS

1. Martin Luther King, Jr., "Speech at SMU" Transcript of speech delivered at Southern Methodist University, Dallas, TX March 17, 1966, https://www.smu.edu/News/2014/mlk-at-smu-transcript-17march1966.

INTRODUCTION: OVERCOMING RELIGION AND RACISM

1. Neil T. Anderson, *Living Free In Christ* (Ventura, CA: Regal Books, 1993), pp.56-58.

CHAPTER 1—OVERCOMERS: OUR JOURNEY TO FREEDOM

1. *The Steps To Freedom in Christ* (Bethany House Publishers) written by Neil T. Anderson is a repentance process that is being used all over the world to help Christians resolve their personal and spiritual conflicts.

CHAPTER 2—OVERCOMING IDENTITY CRISIS

1. Neil T. Anderson, *Victory Over the Darkness* (Bloomington, MN: Bethany House Publishers, 2020).

2. *NASB Study Bible* (Grand Rapids, Michigan: Zondervan Corporation, 1999), p. 10.

3. Alexander Balmain Bruce, *The Training of the Twelve*, 2nd edition (New Canaan, Connecticut: Keats Publishing, Inc., 1979), p. 69.

4. Watchmen Nee, as quoted in *Becoming a Disciple-Making Church* by Neil T. Anderson (Bloomington, MN: Bethany House Publishers, 2016), pp. 29.

5. Neil T. Anderson, *Victory Over the Darkness*, (Bloomington, MN: Bethany House Publishers, 2020), pg. 41

CHAPTER 3—OVERCOMING THE BATTLE FOR THE MIND

1. Watchman Nee, *Secrets to Spiritual Power* (New Kensington, PA: Whitaker House, 1999).

2. Neil T. Anderson, *Becoming a Disciple-Making Church* (Bloomington, MN: Bethany House Publishers, 2016), pp. 35-37.

3. Psychology Tools, "What is CBT?" PsychologyTools.com, accessed on January 27, 2022, https://www.psychologytools.com/self-help/what-is-cbt/.

4. The definition and any facts about the word "noema" come from Neil T. Anderson's book, *Victory Over the Darkness* (Bloomington, MN: Bethany House Publishers, 2000, 2020), chapter 9.

CHAPTER 4—DISCIPLESHIP COUNSELING

1. *Care for the Soul*, edited by Mark R. McMinn & Timothy R. Philips (Downers Grove, IL: IVP Academic, 2001), pp. 10-11.

2. Ibid.

3. *APA Dictionary of Psychology*, "Psychology," American Psychological Association, accessed January 26, 2022, https://dictionary.apa.org/psychology.

4. Neil T. Anderson, *Becoming a Disciple-Making Church* (Bloomington, MN: Bethany House Publishers, 2016), p. 58.

5. Ibid., p. 60.

CHAPTER 5—A DISCIPLESHIP STRATEGY

1. *The Freedom In Christ Course* is available for purchase online at both our U.S. bookstore, www.freedominchrist.com, and our U.K. bookstore, www.ficm.org.uk.

2. Tramaine Hawkins, "Changed," track 4 on *All My Best To You Vol 2*, EMI Gospel (EGS), 2001, compact disc.

3. Neil T. Anderson, *Becoming a Disciple-Making Church*, (Bloomington, MN: Bethany House Publishers, 2016), p. 76.

4. Ibid., p. 77.

5. Dr. Wayne Grudem, foreword to *Liberating Prayer* by Neil T. Anderson (Eugene, OR: Harvest House Publishers, 2012), p. 5.

6. Anderson and Miller, *Walking In Freedom*, (Bloomington, MN: Bethany House, 2009).

7. For more information on TRANSFORM and CFMU, visit our Freedom in Christ U.S. website: www.ficm.org.

CHAPTER 6—OVERCOMING ANGER

1. Neil T. Anderson, *Becoming a Disciple-Making Church* (Bloomington, MN: Bethany House Publishers, 2016), p. 93.

2. Taken from Alexander Pope, "An Essay on Man: Epistle II", part V., lines 1-4, accessed on January 21, 2022, https://www.poetryfoundation.org/poems/44900/an-essay-on-man-epistle-ii. Lines paraphrased slightly.

3. *The Exorcist*, directed by William Friedkin (Hoya Productions, 1973).

4. *The Passion of the Christ*, directed by Mel Gibson (Icon Productions, 2004).

CHAPTER 7—OVERCOMING ANXIETY DISORDERS

1. Edmund J. Bourne, *The Anxiety and Phobia Workbook, 7th Edition, Revised* (Oakland, CA: Hew Harbinger Publications, Inc., 1995).

2. Edmund J. Bourne, *Healing Fear* (Oakland, CA: New Harbinger Publications, Inc., 1998), p. 2.

3. Ibid., p. 5.

4. Ryan Shepard, "Black American anxiety at all-time high, experts say," ABC News, September 5, 2020, https://abcnews.go.com/US/black-american-anxiety-time-high-experts/story?id=72651176.

5. David G. Benner, *Baker Encyclopedia of Psychology* (Grand Rapids, MI: Baker Book House, 1990), p. 786.

6. "Understand Depression & Anxiety: Facts & Statistics," Anxiety & Depression Association of America, accessed January 25, 2022, https://adaa.org/understanding-anxiety/facts-statistics.

7. Ibid.

8. Neil T. Anderson, *Freedom From Fear* (Eugene, OR: Harvest House Publishers, 1999), pp. 175-176.

9. Jim Elliot, as quoted by Tim Chester, "Jim Elliot was No Fool," Crossway, January 8, 2018, https://www.crossway.org/articles/jim-elliot-was-no-fool/.

CHAPTER 8—OVERCOMING DEPRESSION

1. Virginia Woolf, *The Diary of Virginia Woolf*, Vol. 5: 1936-1941, edited by Anne Oliver Bell and Andrew McNeillie (New York: Harvourt, Brace, Jovanocich, 1984), p. 226.

2. Brandi Koskie and Crystal Raypole, "Depression Facts and Statistics" Healthline.com, last updated January 14, 2022, https://www.healthline.com/health/depression/facts-statistics-infographic#prevalence.

3. Michael Burlingame, *The Inner World of Abraham Lincoln* (Illinois: University of Illinois Press, 1997).

4. Ibid., p. 40.

5. Ibid., p. 100.

6. Richard Harrington, "Crushed Velvet," Washington Post, July 9, 1998, https://www.washingtonpost.com/wp-srv/style/features/janetjack.htm.

7. "Black Community: ADAA Board of Directors Statement", Anxiety & Depression Association of America, June 4, 2020, https://adaa.org/find-help/by-demographics/black-community.

8. Neil T. Anderson, *Becoming a Disciple-Making Church* (Bloomington, MN: Bethany House Publishers, 2016), p. 124.

9. Neil T. Anderson, *Becoming a Disciple-Making Church* (Bloomington, MN: Bethany House Publishers, 2016), p. 134.

10. Archibald Hart, *Counseling the Depressed* (Waco, TX: Word Books, 1987), p. 99.

11. Daniel Goleman, *Emotional Intelligence*, as quoted in Mitch and Susan Golant, *What to do When Someone You Love is Depressed* (New York: Villard Books, 1996), p. 23.

12. Neil T. Anderson, *Becoming a Disciple-Making Church* (Bloomington, MN: Bethany House Publishers, 2016), p. 143.

CHAPTER 9—OVERCOMING SEXUAL STRONGHOLDS

1. NCHHSTP Newsroom, "CDC estimates 1 in 5 people in the U.S. have a sexually transmitted infection" Center for Disease Control, January 25, 2021, https://www.cdc.gov/nchhstp/newsroom/2021/2018-STI-incidence-prevalence-estimates-press-release.html.

2. Jeremy Wiles, "15 Mind-Blowing Statistics About Pornography and the Church," Conquer Series, summary of the results from *The Porn Phenomenon* survey by Barna Group in 2016, September 12, 2018, https://conquerseries.com/15-mind-blowing-statistics-about-pornography-and-the-church.

3. For more information about David Kyle Foster and Mastering Life Ministries, visit https://www.masteringlife.org/.

4. David Kyle Foster, *Love Hunger: A Harrowing Journey from Sexual Addiction to True Fulfillment* (Minnesota: Chosen Books, 2014).

5. Neil T. Anderson, *Becoming a Disciple-Making Church* (Bloomington, MN: Bethany House Publishers, 2016), p. 149.

6. Marshal Kirk and Hunter Madsen, *After the Ball: How America Will Conquer Its Fear and Hatred of Gays in the '90s* (New York: Doubleday, 1989).

7. Neil Anderson, *Winning the Battle Within* (Eugene, OR: Harvest House Publishers, 2008).

CHAPTER 10—OVERCOMING ADDICTIONS

1. National Survey of Drug Use and Health (NSDUH), "Highlights for the 2020 NSDUH Annual National Report," Substance Abuse and Mental Health Services Administration (SAMHSA), October 25, 2021, https://www.samhsa.gov/data/release/2020-national-survey-drug-use-and-health-nsduh-releases.

2. Katelyn Newman, "Obesity in America: A Public Health Crisis," U.S. News, September 19, 2019, https://www.usnews.com/news/healthiest-communities/articles/2019-09-19/obesity-in-america-a-guide-to-the-public-health-crisis.

3. Matt Berry, "3 Reasons Why The DARE Program Failed," American Addiction Centers, February 9, 2021, https://americanaddictioncenters.org/blog/why-the-dare-program-failed.

4. The 12-Step Program of Alcoholics Anonymous was based on 6 principles from the Oxford group, a Christian organization founded by Frank Buchman made up of a group of people who had surrendered their lives to God. For more information on the history of the 12 Steps, see article "A history of the 12 Steps" by Cornerstone of Recovery, September 19, 2018, https://www.cornerstoneofrecovery.com/better-way-of-life-a-history-of-the-12-steps/.

5. American Addiction Centers Editorial Staff, "Drug Relapse," American Addiction Centers, Inc., last updated on January 4, 2022, https://drugabuse.com/addiction/relapse/.

6. Neil T. Anderson, *Becoming a Disciple-Making Church* (Bloomington, MN: Bethany House Publishers, 2016), Chapter 9: Overcoming Chemical Addictions.

7. This chart is found in the book *Freedom from Addiction*. Neil T. Anderson and Mike & Julia Quarles, *Freedom from Addiction*, Bloomington, MN: Bethany House Publishers, 1996).

8. For more information on Alcoholics Anonymous (A.A.) and their process, visit their website www.aa.org.

CHAPTER 11—OVERCOMING BROKEN MARRIAGES

1. Stephanie Kramer, "U.S. has world's highest rate of children living in single-parent households," Pew Research Center, December 12, 2019, https://www.pewresearch.org/fact-tank/2019/12/12/u-s-children-more-likely-than-children-in-other-countries-to-live-with-just-one-parent/.

2. Ta-Nehisi Coates, "The math on Black out of wedlock births," The Atlantic, February 17, 2009, https://www.theatlantic.com/entertainment/archive/2009/02/the-math-on-black-out-of-wedlock-births/6738/.

3. Neil T. Anderson, *Becoming a Disciple-Making Church* (Bloomington, MN: Bethany House Publishers, 2016), p. 191.

4. Neil T. Anderson, Marriagetrac, from *Experiencing Christ Together* by Neil T. Anderson and Charles Mylander (Regal Books, 2006), accessed on January 21, 2022 https://www.marriagetrac.com/marriage-license-a-learners-permit/.

5. Ibid.

6. The three types of love are found in Strong's Exhaustive Concordance. James Strong, *Strong's Exhaustive Concordance of the Bible* (Carol Stream, IL: Hendrickson Publishing Group, 2009).

7. The word "possess" in this passage means "to acquire." It is found in the Septuagint and other literature written at the time of Christ and refers to marrying a wife. The word "vessel" is never used anywhere else in the Bible to mean "body." It is translated as "wife" in 1 Peter 3:7. The Hebrew equivalent (keli) of "vessel" means "wife" in rabbinical writings.

Daryl and Stephanie Fitzgerald have a great love for marriage and family. They believe a healthy marriage creates a healthy home environment that promotes the development of healthy children. They are the proud parents of five children: Ashley, Shayna, Darius, Alexis, and Alexandria. With the extensive training they received from Freedom in Christ Ministries, Daryl and Stephanie have had the opportunity to be a part of bringing spiritual, emotional, and mental healing to the body of Christ. Daryl received his Bachelor of Science degree in Psychology & Human Behavior from Liberty University. He became an LCI certified professional life coach through The Life Coach Institute as a mentor and a motivator to help individuals get FIT (Focused, Identify goals, Track their progress) to becoming the best version of who God created them to be. Stephanie completed the Apollos Training Course through the Bible Training Centre for Pastors and Church Leaders.

Daryl and Stephanie have worked closely together for over thirty years giving biblical counsel, coaching, leadership development, and and discipleship training to churches, organizations, and individuals throughout the country, from church leaders to professional athletes. They also participated in filming a 10-week long discipleship course titled the *Freedom in Christ Course* focused on helping individuals understand their identity as children of God. *From Slavery to Freedom*, written with Dr. Neil T. Anderson, is their first book, telling their journey of how they overcame spiritual, mental and emotional wounds from their past. Their desire is for all of God's children to learn the truth of Scripture and become all that Christ designed them to be.

Can We Help You Make Fruitful Disciples?

A church with growing, fruitful disciples of Jesus is a growing, fruitful church that is making a real difference in the community where God has placed it. A key question for church leaders is: "How can I help our people become mature, fruitful disciples as quickly as possible so that they go out and make a real impact?"

A fundamental part of the answer is to help them understand the principles that underlie all of Freedom In Christ's discipleship resources:

- TRUTH—Know who you are in Christ.

- TURNING—Ruthlessly close any doors you've opened to the enemy through past sin and don't open any more.

- TRANSFORMATION—Renew your mind to the truth of God's Word (which is how you will be transformed).

Freedom In Christ has equipped hundreds of thousands of church leaders around the world to use this "identity-based discipleship" approach. As churches base their discipleship around these principles, they report not only changed individual lives but whole changed churches. When churches start to look less like hospitals, full of those who are constantly struggling with their own issues, and more like part of the Bride of Christ, they make an increasing impact on their community.

Our mission is to equip the Church to transform the nations by providing church leaders with transformational discipleship resources that can be used right across their church. Some are specially tailored to the communication styles of different groups such as young people and millennials. Others build on our main Freedom In Christ Course. You can see some of them on the following pages.

Our heart is to help church leaders develop a long-term, whole-church discipleship strategy. Our offices and Representatives around the world run training courses and have people on the ground who like nothing better than to discuss discipleship with church leaders. If you think we can help you in any way as you look to make fruitful disciples, please get in touch.

Find your local office at **www.FreedominChrist.org**

Take Hold Of The Freedom That Is Yours In Christ!

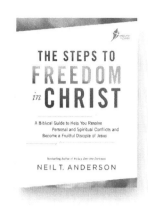

- Do you want to become an even more fruitful disciple of Jesus?

- Are you tired of not fulfilling your full potential as a Christian?

All Christians need to come to know and understand their identity, position and authority in Christt. Knowing those truths helps a believer in Jesus become a growing, fruitful disciple (follower) of Christ. Dr. Neil T. Anderson has been greatly gifted by God to present the biblical truths of our identity and freedom in Christ in a wonderful God-directed, liberating way. These truths are described in the books *Victory Over the Darkness*, and *The Bondage Breaker* which became the foundation of Freedom in Christ Ministries. But this teaching did not originate with Dr. Anderson, it is straight from the New Testament and is new covenant Christianity brought to us initially by the apostles Paul, Peter and John and further developed by the early Church fathers.

The Steps to Freedom in Christ is a biblically-based ministry tool which is derived from James 4:7—"Submit to God, resist the devil and he will flee from you." It is a gentle process of following the Holy Spirit's prompting to deal with the effects of any sin committed by you or against you.

Going through *The Steps to Freedom in Christ* is taking personal responsibility for your life and spiritual growth. It is a systematic approach of examining your heart and life before the Lord and asking Him to reveal areas of your life where there are unresolved sin issues in the light of Scripture. Accordingly, you choose to confess, repent and renounce whatever is standing between you and your spiritual freedom, identify lies believed, and replace them with God's truth.

The Freedom In Christ Course

Now in its third edition and translated into well over 30 languages, *The Freedom In Christ Course* can transform the way you help Christians become fruitful disciples. Focused on firstly establishing every Christian in the sure foundation of their identity in Jesus, it gives them the tools to break free and stay free from all that holds them back, and a strategy for ongoing transformation. It has ten teaching sessions presented by Steve Goss, Nancy Maldonado, and Daryl Fitzgerald plus *The Steps To Freedom In Christ* ministry component presented by Steve Goss and Neil Anderson.

With a specially designed app, extra teaching films, a worship album, Leader's Guide, Participant's Guide, and tons of extras, *The Freedom In Christ Course* offers you everything you need to make disciples who bear fruit that will last!

WHAT PEOPLE ARE SAYING:

"Men, women, and middle and high school students have been radically transformed."—BOB HUISMAN, *Pastor, Immanuel Christian Reformed Church, Hudsonville, MI, USA*

"I recommend it highly to anyone serious about discipleship."
—CHUAH SEONG PENG, *Senior Pastor, Holy Light Presbyterian Church, Johor Baru,Malaysia*

"The Freedom In Christ Course changed me and put me in a position to minister to people in a much more effective way."
—FRIKKIE ELSTADT, *Every Nation Patria, Mossel Bay, South Africa*

"Our chrch has changed as a result of this course. Those who come to Christ and who do the course end up with a rock-solid start to their faith."
—PASTOR SAM SCOTT, *Eltham Baptist Church, Australia*

disciple—FIC's Message For The Millennial Generation

Church leaders report that discipling those in their 20s and 30s is one of their biggest challenges.

disciple is a powerful tool to help you. It speaks the language of 20s and 30s and invites them to dive into the greatest story ever told, God's story. They will learn how to take hold of their freedom and discover their purpose.

- 10 sessions designed to run for approximately 90 minutes each.

- Impactful Starter Films introduce the theme for each session.

- Extra films (via the app) on topics including sex, the occult, and fear.

- Chat and Reflect times allow teaching to take root.

- App with extra teaching films, daily devotional, daily nuggets of extra teaching, and Stronghold–Buster-Builder with reminders.

WHAT PEOPLE ARE SAYING:

"Thank you so much for caring enough to do this. You have no idea how much it means to us that you have taken the time to understand and help us overcome all the stuff that comes at us."

"You really get us and understand us, you don't patronize us and talk down to us."

"God is doing incredible things in the young people at our church and I'm just grateful this course has been able to facilitate that."

"*disciple* is really user-friendly. The young adults really engaged and there were definite light bulb moments."

The Grace Course

If you don't first know God's love for you in your heart—not just your head—it's impossible for your life to be motivated by love for Him. Instead, you are likely to end up motivated more by guilt or shame or fear or pride. You

may be doing all the "right" things, believing all the right things and saying all the right things, but there will be precious little fruit.

Six sessions plus *The Steps to Experiencing God's Grace*:

- Present it yourself or use the video presentations.

- Video testimonies illustrating the teaching points, practical exercises, times of listening to God, and Pause For Thought times.

- Works especially well as a course during Lent.

WHAT PEOPLE ARE SAYING:

"For the first time in the decades that I've been a Christian, I'm suddenly 'getting' grace—it's amazing and it's shocking!"

"I realized that it's not about my performance—He just wants my heart."

"It was AMAZING! During the last session after we had finished nobody moved for what seemed like ages. When the silence eventually did break, people began to spontaneously share all that the course had meant to them. Testimonies to what the Lord had done just flowed out, some were life- changing."

"The Grace Course does a marvelous job in introducing the concept of grace in a simple, engaging and, at times, even humorous way. It is short and to the point, taking an incredibly deep theological issue and making it understandable and practical."

The Lightbringers For Children

The Lightbringers is a powerful resource for churches and parents to use with 5-to-11-year-olds. It is designed to equip them to become fruitful disciples who stay connected to Jesus into their adult lives. They will understand:

- Who they are in Jesus.

- What they have in Jesus.

- How to become fruitful disciples who follow Jesus closely.

It consists of ten action-packed sessions plus specially written versions of *The Steps To Freedom In Christ* ministry component and has versions for two age groups (5-8 and 9-11). It's great for churches, Bible clubs, and families.

The Church Edition includes a comprehensive 276-page Leader's Guide plus downloadable videos, songs, activity sheets, and PowerPoint presentations. The Family Edition is an online-only version designed to be delivered in the home.

WHAT PEOPLE ARE SAYING:

"Parents, educators, children's leaders, and pastors rejoice! There is no longer a void in quality children's curriculum that instills the essentials of identity in Christ and freedom in Christ."

"*The Lightbringers* is a fantastic resource to help children know their identity in Christ and how to view the rest of the world through that lens."

"It has awesome content, is easy to follow, and will fill what has been a huge gap in kids' ministry up to this time."

Freed To Lead

Freed To Lead is a 10-week discipleship course for Christians who are called to leadership—whether in the marketplace, public service, the Church or any other context. It will transform your leadership, free you from drivenness and burnout, enable you to survive personal attacks, use conflict positively, and overcome other barriers to effective leadership.

- Ten sessions plus *Steps to Freedom for Leaders*
- Video testimonies and Pause For Thought discussion times
- Ideal for church leadership teams before rolling out across the church

WHAT PEOPLE ARE SAYING:

"The *Freed To Lead* course has been the most amazing leadership development experience of my career, having been called to both marketplace and church leadership for over 20 years. It dispels worldly leadership myths and practices and provides Biblical foundations for Godly leadership. I whole- heartedly recommend this course for anyone who aspires or is currently called to Godly servant-hearted leadership in any arena."

"An outstanding course—inspirational and motivational, affirming and encouraging."

"It has reinforced my conviction that my identity is first and foremost in Christ, whatever leadership role I may hold."

FREEDOMSTREAM

On-Demand Videos For Our Courses

You can access all of our video material for small group studies online for one low monthly subscription. Try it for free!

Access to all the main Freedom In Christ small group courses so you can browse or use the entire range including:

- *The Freedom In Christ Course*
- *The Lightbringers* – Freedom In Christ For Children
- Freedom In Christ For Young People
- *disciple* (the Freedom In Christ message for 18s to 30s)
- *The Grace Course*
- *Freed To Lead*
- *Keys To Health, Wholeness, & Fruitfulness.*

Free video training courses for course leaders and their teams:

- Making Fruitful Disciples—the Biblical principles of discipleship
- Helping Others Find Freedom In Christ.

No need to buy several DVD sets if you have multiple groups running. Access is for all members of your church so participants can catch up if they miss a session.

For further information, pricing, and to start your free trial go to: FreedomInChrist.org/FreedomStream

FREEDOM IN CHRIST BOOKS

Victory Over the Darkness (Bethany House, 2000). With more than 1,400,000 copies in print, this core book explains who you are in Christ, how to walk by faith in the power of the Holy Spirit, how to be transformed by the renewing of your mind, how to experience emotional freedom, and how to relate to one another in Christ.

The Bondage Breaker (Harvest House Publishers, 2000). With more than 1,400,000 copies in print, this book explains spiritual warfare, what our protection is, ways that we are vulnerable, and how we can live a liberated life in Christ.

Discipleship Counseling (Bethany House, 2003) combines the concepts of discipleship and counseling and teaches the practical integration of theology and psychology helping Christians resolve their personal and spiritual conflicts through genuine repentance and faith in God.

The Steps to Freedom in Christ and the companion interactive video (Bethany House, 2017) are discipleship counseling tools that help Christians resolve their personal and spiritual conflicts through genuine repentance and faith in God.

Restored (Freedom in Christ) is an expansion of the *The Steps to Freedom in Christ* with additional explanation and instruction. Available as an interactive e-book at Restored.pub

Walking In Freedom (Bethany House, 2009) is a 21-day devotional often used for follow-up after processing *The Steps to Freedom in Christ.*

The Bondage Breaker DVD Experience (Harvest House, 2011) is a discipleship course for Sunday school classes and small groups. The lessons are 15 minutes long. It has a companion interactive workbook, but no leaders guide.

SPECIALIZED BOOKS

The Bondage Breaker, The Next Step (Harvest House, 2011) includes several testimonies of people who found their freedom from all kinds of problems, with commentary by Dr. Anderson. It is an important learning tool for encouragers and gives hope to those who are entangled in sin.

Overcoming Addictive Behavior with Mike Quarles (Bethany House, 2003) explores the path to addiction and how a Christian can overcome addictive behaviors.

Overcoming Depression with Joanne Anderson (Bethany House, 2004) explores the nature of depression, which is a body, soul, and spirit problem and presents a wholistic answer for overcoming this "common cold" of mental illnesses.

Daily in Christ with Joanne Anderson (Harvest House, 2000) is a popular daily devotional read by thousands of internet subscribers every day.

Who I Am in Christ (Bethany House, 2001) has 36 short chapters describing who believers are in Christ and how their deepest needs are met in Him.

Freedom from Addiction with Mike and Julia Quarles (Bethany House, 1996) begins with Mike and Julia's journey into addiction and codependency and explains the nature of chemical addictions and how to overcome them in Christ.

One Day at a Time with Mike and Julia Quarles (Bethany House, 2000) is a 120-day devotional helping those who struggle with addictive behaviors and explaining how to discover the grace of God on a daily basis.

Letting Go of Fear with Rich Miller (Harvest House Publishers, 2018) explains the nature of fear, anxiety and panic attacks and how to overcome them.

Setting Your Church Free with Charles Mylander (Bethany House, 2014) explains servant leadership and how the leadership of a church can resolve corporate conflicts through corporate repentance.

Setting Your Marriage Free with Charles Mylander (Bethany House, 2014) explains God's divine plan for marriage and the steps that couples can take to resolve their difficulties.

Christ-Centered Therapy with Terry and Julianne Zuehlke (Zondervan, 2000) explains the practical integration of theology and psychology for professional counselors and provides them with Biblical tools for therapy.

Managing Your Anger with Rich Miller (Harvest House, 2018) explains the nature of anger and how to put away all anger, wrath, and malice.

Grace That Breaks the Chains with Rich Miller and Paul Travis (Harvest House, 2014) explains the bondage of legalism and how to overcome it by the grace of God.

Winning the Battle Within (Harvest House, 2008) shares God's standards for sexual conduct, the path to sexual addiction and how to overcome sexual strongholds.

Rough Road to Freedom (Monarch Books, 2012) is Dr. Anderson's memoir.

The Power of Presence (Monarch Books, 2016) is about experiencing the presence of God during difficult times and what our presence means to each other. This book is written in the context of Dr. Anderson caring for his wife, who was slowly dying with agitated dementia.

For more information or to purchase the above materials, contact Freedom in Christ Ministries:

Canada: www.ficm.ca
UK: www.ficm.org.uk
US: www.ficm.org
International: www.freedominchrist.org

FREEDOM
IN CHRIST

GET IN TOUCH

Freedom In Christ exists to equip the Church to make fruitful disciples who make a real impact in their community. Our passion is to help church leaders develop a discipleship strategy right across their church that will be effective for years to come. How can we help your church?

We offer:

A series of introductory and training events for church leaders.

Advice on establishing a discipleship strategy for your church built around our discipleship resources.

Training and equipping for those in your church who will be involved in implementing that strategy.

For contact details of Freedom In Christ in your country or to find out how to order our resources, go to: FreedomInChrist.org

JOIN US!

If, like us, you are excited about seeing this message of "Truth, Turning, and Transformation" spread throughout the Church around the world, please join us.

JOIN OUR TEAM OF INTERNATIONAL SUPPORTERS

Freedom In Christ exists to equip the Church worldwide to make fruitful disciples. We rely heavily for financial support from people who have understood how important it is to give leaders the tools that will enable them to help people become fruitful disciples, not just converts, especially when we are opening up an office in a new country. Typically, your support will be used to:

- create new resources such as this one
- help establish new Freedom In Christ offices around the world
- translate our resources into other languages
- partner with other organizations worldwide to equip leaders
- equip church leaders around the world.

JOIN THE TEAM OF SUPPORTERS IN YOUR COUNTRY.

We are passionate about working with those who have themselves been touched by the Biblical message of freedom. Financial support enables us to develop new resources and get them into the hands of more church leaders. As a result, many, many people are connecting with this life- changing message. There are always new projects—small and large—that don't happen unless there's funding.

To find out how to support Freedom in Christ in your country, go to FreedomInChrist.org/friends. To support the work of Freedom in Christ in the U.S., go to ficm.org/donate/